BUILDING
HISTORY
SERIES

ALCATRAZ

TITLES IN THE BUILDING HISTORY SERIES INCLUDE:

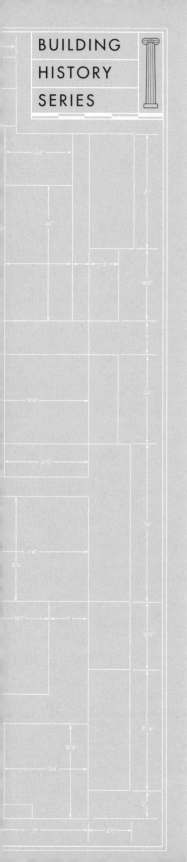

ALCATRAZ

by James Barter

Lucent Books, Inc., San Diego, California

Library of Congress Cataloging-in-Publication Data

Barter, James, 1946–
    Alcatraz / by James Barter.
        p.   cm. — (Building history series)
    Includes bibliographical references and index.
    Summary: Discusses the history of California's Alcatraz island
covering its use as a military prison, as a national maximum
security facility, the lives of prisoners and guards, and its cur-
ent status as a national park.

    ISBN 1-56006-596-6 (lib. : alk. paper)

    1. United States Penitentiary, Alcatraz island, California—His-
tory—Juvenile literature.   2. Prisons—California—Alcatraz Island—Juvenile literature. 3. Alcatraz island (Calif.)—History Juvenile Literature. [1. United States Penitentiary, Alcatraz island,
California—History. 2. Prisons—History. 3. Alcatraz island
(Calif.)—History.] I. Title.   II. Series.
HV9474.A4B37   2000
365'.979461—dc21   99-30280
                                                                        CIP

Copyright 2000 by Lucent Books, Inc.
P.O. Box 289011, San Diego, California, 92198-9011

                    Printed in the U.S.A.

CONTENTS

FOREWORD

Throughout history, as civilizations have evolved and prospered, each has produced unique buildings and architectural styles. Combining the need for both utility and artistic expression, a society's buildings, particularly its large-scale public structures, often reflect the individual character traits that distinguish it from other societies. In a very real sense, then, buildings express a society's values and unique characteristics in tangible form. As scholar Anita Abromovitz comments in her book *People and Spaces*, "Our ways of living and thinking—our habits, needs, fear of enemies, aspirations, materialistic concerns, and religious beliefs—have influenced the kinds of spaces that we build and that later surround and include us."

That specific types and styles of structures constitute an outward expression of the spirit of an individual people or era can be seen in the diverse ways that various societies have built palaces, fortresses, tombs, churches, government buildings, sports arenas, public works, and other such monuments. The ancient Greeks, for instance, were a supremely rational people who originated Western philosophy and science, including the atomic theory and the realization that the earth is a sphere. Their public buildings, epitomized by Athens's magnificent Parthenon temple, were equally rational, emphasizing order, harmony, reason, and above all, restraint.

By contrast, the Romans, who conquered and absorbed the Greek lands, were a highly practical people preoccupied with acquiring and wielding power over others. The Romans greatly admired and readily copied elements of Greek architecture, but modified and adapted them to their own needs. "Roman genius was called into action by the enormous practical needs of a world empire," wrote historian Edith Hamilton. "Rome met them magnificently. Building tremendous, indomitable, amphitheaters where eighty thousand could watch a spectacle, baths where three thousand could bathe at the same time."

In medieval Europe, God heavily influenced and motivated the people, and religion permeated all aspects of society, molding people's worldviews and guiding their everyday actions. That spiritual mindset is reflected in the most important medieval structure—the Gothic cathedral—which, in a sense, was a model of heavenly cities. As scholar Anne Fremantle so elegantly phrases it, the cathedrals were "harmonious elevations of stone and glass reaching up to heaven to seek and receive the light [of God]."

Our more secular modern age, in contrast, is driven by the realities of a global economy, advanced technology, and mass communications. Responding to the needs of international trade and the growth of cities housing millions of people, today's builders construct engineering marvels, among them towering skyscrapers of steel and glass, mammoth marine canals, and huge and elaborate rapid transit systems, all of which would have left their ancestors, even the Romans, awestruck.

In examining some of humanity's greatest edifices, Lucent Books' Building History Series recognizes this close relationship between a society's historical character and its buildings. Each volume in the series begins with a historical sketch of the people who erected the edifice, exploring their major achievements as well as the beliefs, customs, and societal needs that dictated the variety, functions, and styles of their buildings. A detailed explanation of how the selected structure was conceived, designed, and built, to the extent that this information is known, makes up the majority of the volume.

Each volume in the Lucent Building History Series also includes several special features that are useful tools for additional research. A chronology of important dates gives students an overview, at a glance, of the evolution and use of the structure described. Sidebars create a broader context by adding further details on some of the architects, engineers, and construction tools, materials, and methods that made each structure a reality, as well as the social, political, and/or religious leaders and movements that inspired its creation. Useful maps help the reader locate the nations, cities, streets, and individual structures mentioned in the text; and numerous diagrams and pictures illustrate tools and devices that bring to life various stages of construction. Finally, each volume contains two bibliographies, one for student research, the other listing works the author consulted in compiling the book.

Taken as a whole, these volumes, covering diverse ancient and modern structures, constitute not only a valuable research tool but also a tribute to the human spirit, a fascinating exploration of the dreams, skills, ingenuity, and dogged determination of the great peoples who shaped history.

IMPORTANT DATES
IN THE BUILDING OF ALCATRAZ

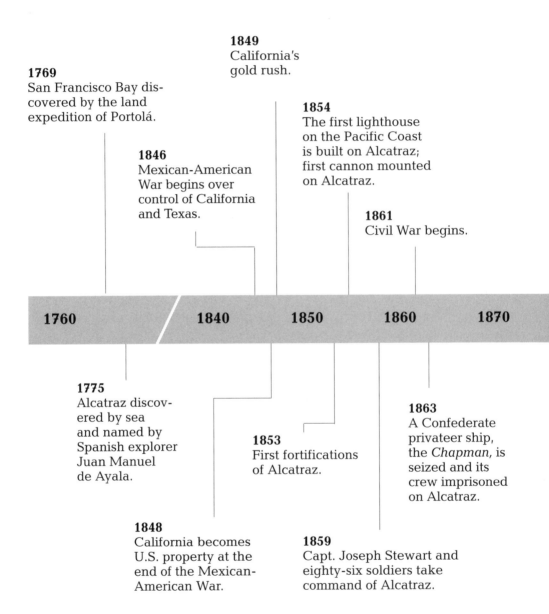

1849
California's
gold rush.

1769
San Francisco Bay dis-
covered by the land
expedition of Portolá.

1854
The first lighthouse
on the Pacific Coast
is built on Alcatraz;
first cannon mounted
on Alcatraz.

1846
Mexican-American
War begins over
control of California
and Texas.

1861
Civil War begins.

1760   1840   1850   1860   1870

1775
Alcatraz discov-
ered by sea
and named by
Spanish explorer
Juan Manuel
de Ayala.

1853
First fortifications
of Alcatraz.

1863
A Confederate
privateer ship,
the *Chapman*, is
seized and its
crew imprisoned
on Alcatraz.

1848
California becomes
U.S. property at the
end of the Mexican-
American War.

1859
Capt. Joseph Stewart and
eighty-six soldiers take
command of Alcatraz.

1934
Alcatraz is made a maximum-security federal penitentiary.

1972
Alcatraz designated as National Park Service site.

1912
Completion of the main cellhouse.

1946
The bloodiest escape attempt ever costs five inmates and two guards their lives.

| 1900 | 1920 | 1940 | 1960 | 1980 |

1915
Alcatraz officially becomes a military prison.

1969
Nineteen-month occupation by American Indian tribes begins.

Alcatraz island

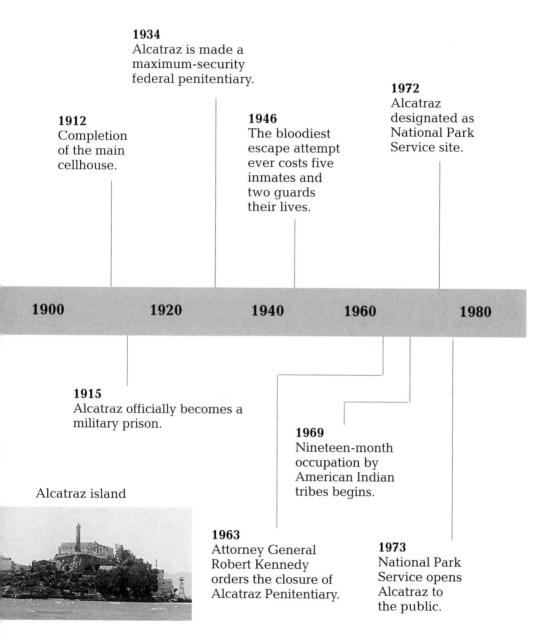

1963
Attorney General Robert Kennedy orders the closure of Alcatraz Penitentiary.

1973
National Park Service opens Alcatraz to the public.

INTRODUCTION

Located in San Francisco Bay, one and a half miles off Fisherman's Wharf and three miles east of the Golden Gate Bridge, the island of Alcatraz straddles the middle of the bay. Once regarded as a rocky outcrop of little commercial or strategic value, it later gained its reputation as a federal penitentiary where disreputable criminals lived desolate lives in brutal contrast to the sweet life of San Francisco. Today open to the public as a national park, Alcatraz is visited annually by over a million tourists who explore and gawk at the steel cells that once caged some of the most notorious felons in the history of the United States.

Scarcely twenty-two acres in size, Alcatraz is one of a few islands that dot the picturesque San Francisco Bay. For centuries its battleship profile attracted relatively little attention, until three sealed train cars filled with federal prisoners secretly arrived there by ferry in 1934.

Later called "the Rock" by inmates housed there, Alcatraz was originally nothing but a rocky island deemed unusable for commercial and industrial use.

Two Alcatraz guards survey a cell block. These correctional officers kept watch over some of the most dangerous men in the United States.

In its function as a maximum-security prison, the dreary isolation of this shadowy island quickly earned it the name by which it is known to millions today—the Rock. Jutting dramatically from the waters of the bay, its jagged cliffs drop to the water so steeply that only one small area is suitable as a landing place. For three decades Alcatraz symbolized the hardened men who languished in its cells: Al "Scarface" Capone, Robert "Birdman" Stroud, Alvin "Creepy" Karpis, George "Machine Gun" Kelly, and a long list of their lesser-known colleagues in crime.

Few human-made structures have inspired the imagination as Alcatraz has done. It is the setting of novels, thrillers, and popular movies and remains a notorious image in the public consciousness. The reality of Alcatraz and how it came into being deserves to be told as well.

EARLY HISTORY

Long before Europeans ever visited, the Native Americans of the coastal Miwok and Ohlone tribes inhabited the hills overlooking Alcatraz and the San Francisco Bay. These Native Americans fished the chilly waters of the bay for shark, striped bass, and the crabs that scuttled across its floor. They hunted deer in the thickly wooded hills and foraged for the wild vegetables and nuts that grew plentifully in the area.

No archaeological evidence exists that these tribes ever inhabited Alcatraz Island, but there is little doubt that they explored it in search of food. Finding bird eggs but no vegetation nor a source of drinking water, they most likely abandoned its harsh rocky landscape in favor of the habitable lands that surround the bay.

A renowned English explorer, Sir Francis Drake, sailed the coast of California twice, missing the entrance to San Francisco Bay both times.

EARLY EXPLORERS

San Francisco Bay, considered by mariners around the globe to be one of the world's great natural harbors, remained beyond the view of early European explorers reconnoitering the coast of California. These early explorers recognized the potential of the vast natural resources of this area. The Portuguese sailor Juan Rodríguez Cabrillo, exploring in the name of the Spanish monarch, sailed north up the California coast in 1542 as far as the border with what today is Oregon and then south back to Mexico but failed both times to discover the entry to the bay. While exploring the California coast, he claimed all the land he saw as a possession of Spain. Following Cabrillo, the Englishman Sir Francis Drake twice missed the Golden Gate, landing instead a few miles north on June 17, 1579, at a small bay that today bears his name, Drake's Bay. Here, before returning south, Drake left evidence of his presence by staking a bronze plaque in a nearby field claiming the land in the name of Queen Elizabeth I. How could these two explorers, and others, have failed to discover the entry to so large and significant a harbor?

Historians speculate that the explorers might have sailed past the entry either at night or in the thick fog that frequently shrouds the Golden Gate. Maritime historians point out that early small wood sailing ships, easily buffeted by unpredictable winds and treacherous currents, forced their captains to sail several miles off the coast of these uncharted waters. Historian Peter Browning adds a novel view to these traditional speculations by pointing out that the geography of San Francisco Bay might have played a part in this saga. Browning believes that from far outside the Golden Gate looking in,

> From most angles, either Angel Island or Alcatraz Island is in the direct line of view, and thus make the opening appear to be a solid coastline. Even when the islands do not conspire to obscure the view into the bay, the crest of the Berkeley hills lines up so well with the sides of the Golden Gate as to create the impression of nothing but land.[1]

THE FIRST EUROPEAN SIGHTING

More than 150 years after Drake's visit, the Spanish, fearing that one of their European rivals for conquest of the New World might attempt to wrest control of California from them, sent both land and sea expeditions to explore and secure the region. For several years, rumors of the existence of the San Francisco Bay had filtered to the Europeans from Indian tribes living in California. A land expedition led by Gaspar de Portolá began 450 miles to the south in San Diego and headed north, discovering San Francisco Bay on November 2, 1769. One of Portolá's men, Miguel Costansó, recorded this event in his diary:

> Several of the soldiers requested permission to go hunting. . . . From the columns of smoke they had noticed all

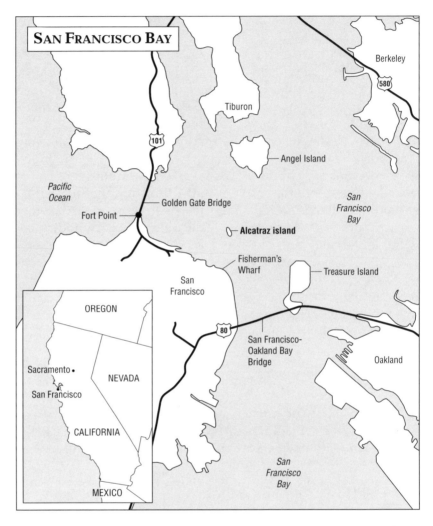

over the level country, there was no doubt that the land must be well populated with natives. This ought to confirm us more and more in the opinion that we were at the port of San Francisco.[2]

Six years after Portolá's discovery of San Francisco Bay by land, the Spanish frigate *San Carlos*, under the command of Juan Manuel de Ayala, made the first recorded entry into San Francisco Bay on August 5, 1775. Ayala scouted the bay for six weeks, charting its waters and coastal geography and noting its desirability as a natural port. He recorded the location of each island in the bay and, noticing the predominance of pelicans

THE BEAR FLAG REVOLT

The decade of the 1840s witnessed the gradual migration of American settlers to California and other Southwest territories then owned by Mexico. This westward expansion was gaining momentum as the United States sought to extend its influence from "sea to shining sea." Although the number of settlers in these outlying Mexican provinces was small, their allegiance was to America and they resisted Mexico's insistence that these territories belonged to her. California, in particular, was a jewel waiting to be claimed, and the Americans were looking for an excuse to act.

In California, rebellious trappers, hunters, and woodsmen led by John Fremont and Kit Carson began the Bear Flag Revolt in the California city of Sonoma, where this loose separatist confederation captured a Mexican fort. In a moment of great bravado, the men ran up a makeshift flag emblazoned with a grizzly bear above the words "California Republic." Following this flourish, they marched to San Francisco where they overwhelmed the Mexican garrison, declared California a republic, and hoisted their flag.

At the same time, unbeknownst to the Bear Flag rebels, Americans living in Texas, a territory also claimed by Mexico, were already in open conflict with the Mexican government. This conflict between the Texans and Mexicans had brought both sides to the brink of war for many years. Finally, in 1846, open warfare erupted in Texas, prompting a declaration of war by the United States against Mexico.

Within one month of the birth of the California Republic, known to the locals as the Bear Flag Revolt, an American warship sailed into the San Francisco Bay and ended the short-lived rebellion by replacing the bear flag with the American flag.

Following two years of war, the peace treaty of Guadalupe Hidalgo set the Rio Grande as the southern boundary of Texas. In exchange for $15 million, Mexico also relinquished its claim to California and other territories.

nesting on one of the islands, named it Isla de los Alcatraces, the Island of Pelicans. In time, the singular form of the word *pelicans* was adopted and the name Alcatraz took hold.

THE MEXICAN-AMERICAN WAR

Although the Spanish expressed interest in exploring and controlling the area around San Francisco Bay, they committed more resources to occupying and controlling southern California and Mexico. For nearly one hundred years after its initial discovery of the bay, Spain spared few soldiers and little equipment to secure this prime piece of property.

With the granting of independence to Mexico, control over California passed from Spain to Mexico, which expressed little more interest in the region until 1838, when Mexico passed a law allowing the governor of California to grant possession of California's coastal islands to qualified Mexican citizens. Under this law, the Mexican governor of California, Pio Pico, granted an American who had become a Mexican citizen, Julian Workman, the right to occupy Alcatraz. The one stipulation Pico imposed on Workman was to build a lighthouse on the island. Once Workman agreed to this condition, Pico handed Alcatraz over.

Although Workman's intentions of constructing a lighthouse may have been genuine at the time, larger historical events intervened. Building tensions between the United States and Mexico finally erupted into open warfare, and on May 13, 1846, the U.S. Congress officially declared war on Mexico.

In June 1846, skirmishes between American settlers and Mexican troops became increasingly frequent and violent in northern California. A group of renegade American settlers led by Kit Carson and John C. Fremont attacked and seized the Mexican garrison in Sonoma, about forty miles north of San Francisco. They declared California independent from Mexico and named it the California Republic. Emboldened by their success, they took their rebellion to San Francisco where they attacked and neutralized the Mexican fort located there.

After its declaration of war against Mexico, the United States sent two warships into San Francisco Bay to secure the area. The war lasted just over two years, ending on May 30, 1848, with all of California under the control of the United States. Also ended was the California Republic. Although Carson and Fremont thought that they had liberated California, the

Until 1848, San Francisco was a relatively obscure town. The discovery of gold in the hills nearby, however, made the city a landmark overnight as thousands rushed to make their fortunes as miners.

commander of the U.S. warships made it clear to them that the United States now owned California.

THE COMING OF THE FORTY-NINERS

With its ownership of California settled, the United States moved to secure its hold on the territory, particularly on the natural harbor of San Francisco Bay. If the importance of San Francisco Bay as a port was not reason enough to protect it from foreign invaders, the discovery in 1848 of gold in the hills just a few days' ride northeast of San Francisco certainly was.

As reports of vast riches spread throughout America and the rest of the world, ships loaded with enthusiastic prospectors bound for California sailed for the closest port to the gold fields—San Francisco. In little more than a year, the population of San Francisco exploded. Historian John Martini makes this observation about the gold rush and the miners, known as Forty-Niners, who flocked there:

GOLD!

Immediately following the Mexican-American War, California remained a relatively quiet area far from the major population centers of America. The East Coast was rapidly developing and the westward migration of settlers was just beginning. Most of the western lands at this time remained within the domain of the Native Americans.

In January 1848, in the little town of Coloma, California, not far from Sacramento, James Marshall discovered gold at Sutter's Mill, changing forever the history of California. Although Marshall only discovered four nuggets initially, news of the discovery quickly spread first to San Francisco, then throughout America, and finally around the world.

Driven by hopes of buying a farm or paying off a large debt, men struck by gold rush fever flooded to California clinging to the fantasy that one year's digging might allow them to realize their dreams

Ready to greet these men in San Francisco and the California gold fields were unscrupulous merchants eager to charge them inflated prices for supplies. Newspaper articles from this era record businessmen buying up every mining tool imaginable like shovels, mining pans, and picks. After they had cornered the market on these mining tools, they raised their prices to astronomical heights, forcing newly arrived miners to pay up to $15 for a mining pan they had bought for fifty cents a few days earlier. Many businessmen pocketed far more money than did the miners.

Two miners pan for gold outside of Sutter's Mill, where gold was first discovered in January of 1848.

Hundreds of thousands of crazed gold seekers joined in the rush, arriving in San Francisco from all over the world by boat. The gold rush continued for several years before the rich veins played out, but the image of California as a place of opportunity still holds true.

San Francisco seemingly grew overnight from a village of 300 people to a metropolis of 35,000. California became the focal point of world attention, and the need for fortifications became of paramount importance to the army. The little-used bay was suddenly, incalculably, valuable.[3]

In short order, as the gold rush brought international fame to San Francisco and California, in 1850 an American military commission set to the task of determining the best defense for San Francisco Bay. Its initial recommendation was to locate a fort at either side of the bay's entry, known as the Golden Gate, each with a battery of heavy cannon. With only one mile of water separating the two forts, military strategists predicted that any ship attempting to run through the defense would suffer a deadly barrage of cannon fire. Fort Point already existed on the southern point of the gate, but building the second fort on the north point would prove to be a more challenging task.

San Francisco in January of 1850, where the population soared in one year from three hundred to thirty-five thousand.

Recognizing that fast ships possibly might slip through the two forts' fire, the commission also designated Alcatraz as a defense site and approved a budget of $300,000 for initial construction of a third fort located there. Alcatraz would prove a welcome beacon to ships whose intentions were friendly, but would present a formidable obstacle to those with hostile intent.

THE ALCATRAZ LIGHTHOUSE

Maritime traffic in the San Francisco Bay experienced unprecedented congestion during the gold rush. This condition, coupled with the notoriously thick San Francisco fog, occasionally caused the wooden ships sailing into the bay to be wrecked on the various islands that obstruct the shipping lanes. In 1852, six years after Pio Pico ordered John Workman to build a lighthouse on Alcatraz, the U.S. government set to the task.

As a safeguard for ships in foul weather, the Mexican government ordered that a lighthouse be built on Alcatraz. The lighthouse was completed by the U.S government in 1854.

Intended as the first of eight lighthouses to dot the treacherous California coast, its design was a copy of lighthouse style in operation on the East Coast of the United States, known as the Cape Cod. Measuring thirty-eight by twenty feet, the Alcatraz lighthouse contained not only the light but also apartments for the families of the two keepers who operated the light around the clock.

Before the lighthouse could be set in place to warn ships of hazards in the San Francisco Bay, a dock was required to offload the tons of material needed for the construction which had to be brought by boat to the island. Most of the island was unsuitable for a dock because of its sheer cliffs. The one suitable spot along the southeast corner had a small cove where engineers built the wharf. From the wharf, crews built a switchback road up to the plateau of the island.

The lighthouse was to be the first structure built on the island, so engineers had their choice of sites. To achieve maximum visibility, they chose the point of highest elevation, near the southern end of the island. The two-story lighthouse looked like a small house with a glass tower, containing the light and lens, protruding from the roof. This tower had a one-foot-thick wall and an inside diameter of eight feet. Atop the tower, architects designed a lookout deck sheathed with copper to protect it from the elements.

The East Coast contractors who built the lighthouse assumed that Californians did not have the necessary materials, tools, or expertise to get the job done. To eliminate the uncertainties of what they thought of as the "wild west," the contracting company dispatched a supply ship to San Francisco that sailed all the way around South America. After a voyage of several months it arrived in San Francisco loaded with most of the materials and tools necessary to build the lighthouse, along with the craftsmen to build it: specialists in concrete work, timber framing, roofing, and the installation of the lens.

The building material included pine flooring, doors, windows, glass, shutters, roofing, hardware, and cupboards. The experienced construction workers quickly completed the dormitory, consisting of bedrooms and kitchens for two families and fireplaces for heating. Installation of the lens for the light, accessed by an iron spiral staircase in the center of the dormitory, was not so simple.

The heart of the lighthouse is the lens, which focuses and magnifies a whale-oil flame on a wick. The key to a good flame was to trim the wick in an arc with the crown at the top gently sloping down at the two ends. The importance of this skill earned the lighthouse keepers the nickname "wickies." The lens then magnified the flame two thousand times. The wickies, who were responsible for replenishing the whale oil, polishing the many prisms of the lens, and trimming the wicks, were paid fifty dollars a month.

The design of the wick is one factor in a light's visibility; the quality of the lens is another. The larger and better quality the crystal prisms of the lens, the better it magnifies and focuses the light and the farther the beam is projected. Experienced lens cutters were a rare breed, and the designers of the Alcatraz lighthouse purchased its lens from the Sautier Company in France.

The lens was called Fresnel style after its French inventor, Augustin Fresnel. It consisted of series of prisms joined within a brass framework to focus the light into a horizontal beam that carried to the horizon. Manufactured in many different sizes, the lens was referred to by its size, or order. A first-order lens stood over twelve feet high; a sixth-order lens stood only sixteen inches. The lens bound for Alcatraz was a third order. On June 1, 1854, at a cost of $15,000, the Alcatraz lighthouse was dedicated and the wick was lit for the first time, projecting a beam of light that could be seen fourteen miles out to sea. With the completion of the lighthouse, the U.S. Army turned its attention to the fortification of the island.

CANNON FOR PELICANS

The military commission's initial recommendation called for construction of two cannon batteries on Alcatraz. The first would be located along the southern cliffs to concentrate fire on ships that might be nearing the city of San Francisco. The second would be placed along the northern cliffs in position to attack ships coming through the Golden Gate as well as ships moving along the north end of the bay. In the end, a third, west-facing battery was added to the plan. With the beginnings of the fortifications, the pelicans and other birds of Alcatraz that had occupied the island for thousands of years fled for new nesting places. Once construction was in full swing, 150 men worked to convert Alcatraz from an island for nesting birds to an island for cannon.

One of 124 total cannon situated around the island for maximum protection against a possible naval assault on San Francisco.

Each of the three batteries had a slightly different configuration depending on its placement and range. North Battery, for example, began with twenty-seven cannon in 1855 but by 1861 the number had expanded to thirty-five, including a mix of light, intermediate, and heavy weaponry. Engineers determined that South Battery, initially consisting of thirty-one cannon, would be set forty feet above the water line. The number of cannon for this battery later rose to thirty-four.

Cannon batteries, to be effective, must sit on level foundations. To accommodate the cannon, engineers set themselves to the task of blasting and leveling terraces on which the cannon would sit. The rock on Alcatraz was not suitable as a building material because it was too brittle to cut into large blocks that could be used for building. Attempts to cut the stone into usable blocks simply shattered the stone. This unfortunate composition forced builders to look elsewhere for building stones. Ferrying building material to Alcatraz for terracing was as difficult as finding it. Alcatraz historian John Martini explains the problem:

Locating suitable building materials was a problem. While some locally quarried granite was available in California, much of the rock had to be imported, some from as far away as China. To add to their supply problems, none of the locally produced brick satisfied the engineers. Most of the samples they tested turned out to be either too weak or the bricks varied widely in their dimensions.[4]

Once workers had completed the terracing, they set to the task of protecting each battery from the guns of enemy ships. To provide protection, masons set sandstone blocks into concrete to form thick protective walls called scarps. These scarp walls were constructed directly in front of the cannon so as to hold the cannon in place and to provide protection from enemy cannon fire. Masons then backfilled rock rubble against the scarps to a depth of fifteen feet and poured concrete over the rubble to within six feet of the top of the scarp. This technique, used on all batteries, created a concrete terrace for the cannon six feet below the top of the scarp so that only the cannon muzzle protruded over the scarp, providing enemy gunners a minimal target. Deep underground, ten feet beneath each battery, workers dug tunnels to provide safe storage for cannon powder, water, and food. With the completion of the tunnels, the terraces were ready for the mounting of the cannon.

One of three cannon batteries around Alcatraz. Workers built huge protective walls around each cannon plus underground tunnels for storing gunpowder.

CREATING A CIRCLE OF FIRE

In 1854 the first 11 cannon arrived on Alcatraz, and within the next seven years the total reached 124. These cannon lined not only the initial north, south, and west batteries but also several additional smaller ones added to complete the circle of fire. To load and fire the weapons, Alcatraz mustered a force of 8 officers and 320 soldiers.

The cannon were called Rodmans, after the man who designed them, and were mounted on concrete platforms on which flat circular steel rails were set to correspond to wheels on the carriages of the cannon. When the cannoneers mounted the cannon, they adjusted the wheels of the cannon to the steel rails. It was the rails that allowed the cannoneers to rotate their weapons into the desired position.

The heavy Rodmans were of three sizes, capable of firing balls six, eight, and ten inches in diameter. Made of solid iron, these balls weighed 27, 64, and 125 pounds, respectively. The largest cannon, capable of firing the ten-inch balls, weighed 10,000 pounds.

The projectiles these cannon fired were of three types: solid shot, incendiary, and exploding. Cannoneers used the solid shot against the thick oak planking of warships. The objectives of using the solid shot were to punch a hole in the ship just below the waterline, causing flooding, or to render the ship dead in the water by destroying the riggings. Incendiary shells were simply solid shot that cannoneers heated in ovens until it was red-hot. The hull of an enemy ship would be set afire on impact with such a shell. Exploding shells were filled with explosives and had wicks that the cannoneers lit before firing. Cannoneers adjusted the length of the wick so the shell would explode in the air, raining shrapnel down on soldiers and sailors below. If the cannoneers set the length of the wick perfectly, the ball exploded fifty to a hundred feet above the target. As the exploding ball arced across the sky toward its target, it left a trail of sparks from the burning wick.

By the mid-1850s, Alcatraz was beginning to take on the profile of a fortress. To accommodate the workers, dozens of small temporary brick buildings were constructed between 1854 and 1856. These buildings included a laborers' barracks capable of housing ninety-six men, a kitchen and mess hall, a water tank, stables, a storehouse for cement and blasting powder, and several small workshops.

In 1857 Congress appropriated another $200,000 to complete the first three batteries as well as a guardhouse. The guardhouse, built near the wharf, was a three-story structure composed of a granite first story and two brick upper stories. The guardhouse included a gun room that housed two heavy guns, a small jail where prisoners could be chained to iron rings in the walls, and a sally port that served as a fortified entryway. This sally port provided a fortified double entry system intended to keep intruders from breaking into the fort. The sally port would be the first line of defense against any invading force that might slip past the fire of the cannon.

THE GAUNTLET TO THE SALLY PORT

Engineers determined that the most vulnerable part of the island for an attack was the wharf on the southeast corner of the island near the laborers' barracks and the guardhouse. To protect this weak point, engineers placed a series of obstacles to repulse an enemy landing force.

The first obstacle leading from the wharf was a fifteen-foot-deep dry moat on the only road leading to the top of the island. Normally a drawbridge spanned the dry moat, but guards could raise it under attack. The second obstacle, the three-story barracks house located on the bluff above the wharf, provided riflemen with an unobstructed firing line to intruders attempting to make their way up the road to the sally port.

The last obstacle to the top of the island was the sally port. Common to most forts during the 1800s, and still in use today in many penitentiaries, the sally port was completed in 1859. The layout of the double door system was rectangular; the front door opened into an enclosed area backed by a rear door.

The two doors of the sally port were constructed of the hardest of woods, solid oak planks, with iron studs embedded in them to withstand ax blows and saw blades. The first door could be unlocked only from the enclosed entry area and the second door could be unlocked only from the outside. The walls of the interior were lined with slits behind which riflemen could fire point-blank on invaders trapped between the two doors. As soon as intruders landed on the wharf, they would need to pass through this gauntlet of defenders culminating with the sally port before gaining access to cannon at the interior of the island.

THE CITADEL

Once the guardhouse and sally port strengthened the island from attack, the need for a permanent soldiers' barracks took precedence. In 1857, construction began on a defensive barracks, called the Citadel. Located on the very top of the island, engineers designed it to be a solid mass capable of withstanding naval bombardments as well as infantry attack.

With this idea in mind, the design called for a three-story structure 112 by 52 feet surrounded by a 20-foot-wide dry moat. Since the moat completely surrounded the entire Citadel, the first floor of the Citadel was recessed 12 feet below the ground. Access to the Citadel, across the moat, was accomplished by two drawbridges that led soldiers to the second floor. To provide adequate internal strength, steel I-beams, a new development in construction technology, were used to support the Citadel. The 4-foot-thick walls were constructed of brick and had rifle slits on the ground floor that were 4 inches wide. At two opposite corners, towers served as gun emplacements in case of an attack. Along the top of the Citadel, a walkway provided soldiers a place to stand and fight off attackers.

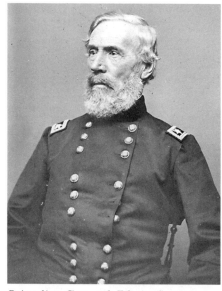

Brigadier General Edwin Sumner assumed command of the fortifications on Alcatraz in April 1861.

Designed as a defensive barracks, the Citadel housed the soldiers. On the ground floor, on the same elevation as the dry moat, were located the kitchens, storage rooms, and four bedrooms. The second floor had additional bedrooms, four dining rooms, a reading room, laundry room, and rooms for quiet relaxation. The top floor was divided into eight officer's bedrooms and servants' quarters. The total budget for the Citadel was $87,689.

Although no enemy force ever tested the sally port or the Citadel, General Edwin Sumner, who assumed command of Alcatraz on April 25, 1861, thought it might soon be tested, when he received news of the start of the Civil War. No longer a fort designed to fight a foreign enemy at some future time, Alcatraz now braced for war against other Americans.

An engineer working with two 15-inch Rodman cannon. At the outbreak of the Civil War, General Sumner placed five of these around the island to ensure safety from Southern loyalists living in the San Francisco area.

THE CIVIL WAR

When news of the outbreak of the Civil War arrived in April 1861, Sumner feared an attack by Southern loyalists living in the San Francisco area. He immediately ordered the Alcatraz garrison to be on full alert and increased its complement of soldiers to 361. The government decided to place heavier cannon on Alcatraz, ordering the appropriation of money to provide five 15-inch Rodmans, at the time the largest cannon made.

Enormous in comparison to the existing ten-inch cannons, the 15-inch Rodmans could hurl a 440-pound iron ball that even at a range of three miles could penetrate the 4-foot-thick oak hulls of warships. Weighing 50,000 pounds, these giant weapons caught everyone's attention. By the end of the Civil War, the cannon of Alcatraz were collectively capable of discharging 6,949 pounds of cannon balls in a single volley.

Alcatraz, its builders hoped, would be an effective part of San Francisco's defenses, but another use of the island was soon to present itself. Sumner caught wind of a conspiracy on the part of Southern sympathizers to raid the arsenal at Alcatraz

and in response placed a ship named the *Chapman* under surveillance. As the *Chapman* made its way to Alcatraz under the
cloak of darkness, soldiers from Alcatraz seized the ship and imprisoned the captain and crew in the small stockade located on
the island. This was the first time that Alcatraz was used as a
prison.

The jailing of the conspirators from the *Chapman* brought to
light the fact that Alcatraz was not only a perfect fort but a perfect prison. Surrounded by bone-chilling water and garrisoned
by several hundred armed soldiers, military planners quickly
identified a secondary function for the island. Once other forts in
the West heard about the secure prison facilities available on the
island, they sent their most violent military prisoners there. The
prisoner population rose from the original fifteen crew members
of the *Chapman* to forty-nine by the time the Civil War ended in
1865.

The end of the Civil War brought a return to normalcy in the
San Francisco Bay area, but the wartime use of Alcatraz as a
military prison had begun to shape the island's destiny.

MILITARY PRISON

Largely isolated from the events of the Civil War, which raged in the East, the armament of Alcatraz was rendered obsolete by technological advances in weaponry, including the development of ironclad ships and improvements in long-range artillery. Moreover, a report detailing the likelihood of cannoneer casualties if enemy shells were to explode on Alcatraz proved worrisome to military planners. Shells fired by enemy ships, it was feared, would explode, sending thousands of fist-size rock fragments showering down on the gunners' positions. With advances in weaponry making the armament on Alcatraz increasingly outmoded, the Army Corps of Engineers drew up plans to radically alter the island's defense.

In 1868, Major George Mendell of the Army Corps of Engineers made the decision to modernize the defenses of Alcatraz. His primary recommendation was to remove all of the brick and rock scarps in favor of sand and earthen versions that could absorb exploding shells without throwing chunks of brick and rock against the cannoneers. To accomplish this, Mendell ordered the leveling of all peaks on the island, the filling of all gulleys, and the use of the excess dirt to replace the rock scarps. About one-half of the prison population having been deemed trustworthy labor, fifty prisoners began excavations in exchange for reduced sentences.

A variety of tools was used to carry out the backbreaking work, including earth carts, rock carts, rock drags, derricks for raising large stones, picks, shovels, and wheelbarrows. With these tools, prisoners moved thousands of tons of rock, dumping it in front of the cannon batteries. When questioned about the usefulness of convict labor, Mendell observed that they were better than nothing:

The men are not industrious and they are careless and at
times malicious in their treatment of public property.
With all these drawbacks, there is some profit in em-
ploying them.[5]

Even with what amounted to slave labor, Mendell estimated
the cost to renovate the defenses of Alcatraz at $323,400, bring-
ing the total cost of fortifying Alcatraz to $1,601,677—more than
five times the original $300,000 budget of 1850.

THE FORT MAKES WAY FOR A PRISON

As the government became increasingly dependent upon prison
labor for the leveling and grading of Alcatraz, the need for better cells to house untrustworthy men also increased. The small,
crude jail built near the sally port before the Civil War gave way
in 1867 to an improved two-story brick jail with cells measuring
3.5 by 6 feet for individual prisoners. Although the new quarters
were an improvement over the old jail, the prisoners still slept
on wooden pallets. As the prison population on Alcatraz continued to grow because of the transfer of high-risk prisoners from
other army forts in the West, more temporary jails went up on
the island. Historian Erwin Thompson makes the following observation:

> Alcatraz island (more by accident than design) was des-
> tined to become the army's first long-time prison. In the
> summer of 1861, the commander of the Department of
> the Pacific, Brig. Gen. Edwin V. Sumner, found an expe-
> dient solution to the problems of the growing numbers of
> military prisoners and of improving military security by
> ordering the transfer of prisoners in the Presidio guard-
> house [on the mainland] to Alcatraz on August 27. Surely,
> no one that day envisioned that this was the first step in
> the 73-year history of military penology on the Rock.[6]

Aside from the island's growing importance as a military
prison, Alcatraz continued to be viewed as an important part of
the nation's defenses. The centennial of the signing of the Declaration of Independence appeared to Mendell to be an ideal occasion for demonstrating the as yet untested firepower of the forts
guarding San Francisco Bay. On the afternoon of July 4, 1876,
Mendell and his high command ordered cannon at Fort Point and

Alcatraz to open fire on an unmanned schooner as a means of proving the effectiveness of the defenses to the viewing public. But after a blistering salvo against the helpless schooner that filled the air with thick acrid smoke, not a single cannonball had found its mark, much to the army's embarrassment. Its confidence in the fort's usefulness as a defensive installation undermined, Congress drastically reduced its funding for Alcatraz.

Mendell, shaken by the congressional lack of faith in Alcatraz, nonetheless continued work on the island's fortifications, forcing the prisoners to slice and level the island and in the process reducing the summit from 125 feet above sea level to a uniform 60 feet. Alcatraz's cannon, he was certain, would be needed someday.

In addition to new armament, Mendell focused the remaining funds on renovations to many of the older secondary buildings on the island, such as the stables, carpentry shops, laborers' barracks, and various storage facilities. In 1880 the army erected three spacious houses near the Citadel for use by the senior officers. Although only their foundations remain, they were

Alcatraz island, 1883. The island became increasingly important as a military prison in the 1860s and 1870s.

DAILY PRISON LIFE IN THE 1860s

However unpleasant or barbaric prison life may have seemed to federal prisoners during the twentieth century, nothing they experienced could compare to the harsher treatment that nineteenth-century prisoners endured on Alcatraz. Lacking central heat, decent medical attention, and attention to reasonable personal needs, the early inmates suffered terribly while imprisoned.

The day began at 5:00 A.M. when guards roused prisoners to wooden mess halls for breakfast followed by a walk to the latrines built on the rocks over San Francisco Bay. This routine was especially arduous during the cold winter months when San Francisco fog is particularly cold and damp.

Following the morning routine, guards led all men considered trustworthy to work areas around the island to excavate rocky areas with pick and shovel. Much of the work consisted of breaking up boulders too large to move into smaller pieces that could be loaded into wheelbarrows for removal to another part of the island. For a few, the best work on the island was constructing wood and brick buildings. Many prisoners found ways to avoid the tedious and backbreaking work by violating prison rules. Daily life for untrustworthy prisoners consisted of menial tasks, such as washing clothes and cleaning buildings, while violent prisoners were confined to their cells for the entire day.

Failure to observe rules often brought corporal punishment in the form of whippings or brandings. Military prisoners convicted of desertion received a brand on the hip with the letter D and those convicted of thievery with the letter T. Within a few years, branding came to be viewed as inhumane by military authorities and the letters were tattooed on the hip instead. Another form of punishment was to isolate a prisoner in the underground storage areas referred to by the prisoners as the "dungeons." Severe cases of rule violations sent the offenders to an iron cage used for solitary confinement.

consistent with the fashionable Victorian style of architecture popular in San Francisco at that time. They were architectural jewels that crowned an otherwise grim architectural reality. Junior officers benefited from remodeling of the interior of the Citadel, providing them with private entrances. Rooms were provided in the basement for use by servants.

The Spanish-American War of 1898 created new fears of a possible invasion of San Francisco, and the army again increased the size of the garrison enormously; the prison population also grew. A prison stockade, consisting of three two-tiered wooden cellhouses known as the Upper Prison, was hastily built on what had been the island's parade ground. A latrine, guardhouse, and a twelve-foot wall with sentry walk completed the expansion of the prison facilities. By 1902, there were 461 military prisoners on the island. The fact that Alcatraz was functioning more as a prison than a fort was becoming increasingly evident.

In the course of the ongoing renovations, the cannon on the island were gradually removed until, by 1901, there were no fully functional artillery pieces remaining on the island. In all its years as a military fort, the weapons on Alcatraz were never fired against an enemy.

A NEAR RIOT

An unlikely event further pushed along the transformation of Alcatraz from a fort to a modern prison. The fact that the army viewed jails and other support buildings as secondary to the primary function of a fort meant that most were built of wood and were intended to be temporary. On January 6, 1902, a kerosene lamp lighting the old wooden cellblock fell from the wall and ignited the wooden floor. Although guards quickly doused the fire, at the first opportunity the inmates rioted because, locked in their cells, they had been at the mercy of the guards, who might or might not have noticed the fire in time to extinguish it. This fire, combined with deteriorating and unsanitary conditions, prompted an audit by the government of the facilities in 1902. Following the audit, the commander of Alcatraz prepared a report stating that the temporary cellhouses were

> rotten and unsafe; the sanitary conditions very dangorous [sic] to health. They are dark and damp, and are fire traps of the most approved kind. Here are confined life, 40, 20, 15 year and lesser term men. *All* must be taken,

three times a day and marched 1/4 mile, through the post, to meals, requiring 16 sentinels. This is a dangerous method, especially in winter, when darkness comes early and daylight comes late. Prisoners have escaped from these marching columns.[7]

As Alcatraz eased into the business of housing military prisoners, the turnover of inmates rose sharply, because Alcatraz now received many petty military criminals for short-term incarceration. A growing inmate population forced the army to allocate more funds for permanent buildings, including a permanent cellhouse.

After the audit's report, work crews began expansion of the Upper Prison in 1904. In addition to the expansion of the cellhouses, they added a kitchen, library, dining room, and bathhouse. By containing all of the prisoner facilities within the walls of the Upper Prison, the capacity expanded and Alcatraz appeared a step closer to being more prison than fort.

In April 1906, the great San Francisco earthquake devastated the city. The ensuing fires consumed much of the city over several days and forced the police to transfer all prisoners in their custody to Alcatraz until the city's jail could be rebuilt. This mixture of both military and civilian prisoners played a major role in the War Department's decision in 1907 to formally abandon the idea of continuing to operate the facility as a fort, opting instead to designate it as a U.S. military prison.

THE 1906 SAN FRANCISCO EARTHQUAKE

On April 18, 1906, a tremendous earthquake rocked northern California. Hardest hit was the city of San Francisco, which was devastated more by the ensuing fires that swept the city than by the earthquake itself. When the earthquake struck at 5:15 A.M., hundreds of buildings in the downtown area collapsed or partially collapsed. Fires broke out shortly after the quake and by 9:00, much of the city was engulfed in flames that leaped from block to block. Fire departments were able to do little more than wait for the fire to burn itself out as water pressure to the hoses fell too low to douse the flames.

THE MODERN CENTRAL CELLHOUSE

With a budget of $250,000 at his disposal, the first commandant of the military prison, Lieutenant Colonel Reuben Turner, directed his energies toward consolidating all of the wooden cellhouses, along with the fifty-year-old three-story brick Citadel, into one central concrete cellhouse. Unlike his predecessors' haphazard approach to constructing the older structures on the island, Turner employed architects to design a state-of-the-art prison reviewed by army engineers to ensure its structural integrity. Designed to house all the prisoners within its walls, the cellhouse also included administrative offices, shower facilities, a mess hall, dining room, library, and a small hospital.

A structure this size required further leveling of the central area at the top of the island and the razing of the fifty-year-old Citadel along with the fifty-five-year-old lighthouse. Some of the materials from the old Citadel were salvaged for use in the new cellhouse. For example, Turner set aside the two beautifully carved gray granite entrances to the Citadel for incorporation

In 1906, the San Francisco earthquake that destroyed much of the city forced police to transfer their prisoners to Alcatraz until the jails could be rebuilt.

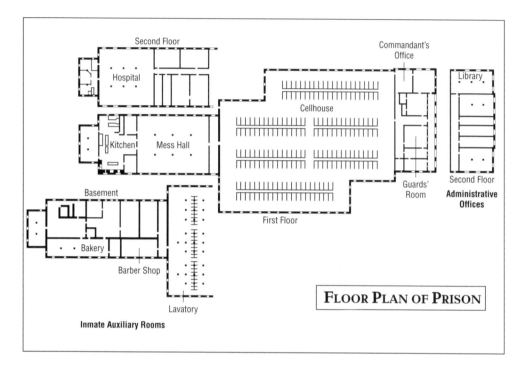

Second Floor

Commandant's Office

Hospital

Library

Cellhouse

Kitchen

Mess Hall

Second Floor

Guards' Room

Administrative Offices

Basement

First Floor

Bakery

Barber Shop

FLOOR PLAN OF PRISON

Lavatory

Inmate Auxiliary Rooms

into the new cellhouse. Hundreds of thousands of bricks were also saved for use throughout the island and several twenty-four-inch by fifty-foot-long steel I-beams found their way into the new building as well.

Army engineers supervised all labor on the project, but because of the difficulty of completing a structure of this size and complexity, civilians provided the skilled labor for the ironwork, riveting of the steel I-beams, laying out of the electrical and water conduits, and plastering. Convict labor contributed to the unskilled work of mixing concrete, building temporary wooden scaffolding, and hauling heavy construction materials.

One of the major problems to be solved was how to protect the new structure from the corrosive effects of the salt air. After the steel I-beams were placed, they were encased in concrete to insulate them from the salt air and to protect them from warping in the unlikely event of fire. Engineers also paid special attention to the composition of the concrete because the salt air constantly swirling around the island could rapidly erode the hard concrete to a soft powder. To retard the deterioration process, freshwater brought to the island in the tanker *El Aquador* was

The outer cellhouse was built with six cell blocks inside, creating a prison within a prison and making escape almost impossible for prisoners incarcerated there.

used in mixing the concrete. In addition to this precaution, structural engineers mixed a waterproofing compound into the wet concrete to prevent saltwater from penetrating after it had dried.

The cellhouse was also designed to resist the incessant cold, wet, foggy air with the installation of interior steam radiators to heat the building in winter. In addition, ventilation was designed to circulate fresh air in the summer. The introduction of modern heating and ventilation systems greatly reduced the incidence of illness among the prisoners and their guards. Furthermore, those prisoners fortunate enough to occupy the two cellblocks facing the windows had the additional good fortune of having the warmest cells as well as the best lit.

The cellhouse, the most dominant structure on the island, was partitioned into three distinct sections: cellblocks in the center, inmate auxiliary rooms on the northern end, and administrative offices on the southern end. This revolutionary design effectively isolated all prisoners in one building for almost all of their activities.

A PRISON WITHIN A PRISON

Turner designed the 480-foot-long cellhouse to contain six hundred inmates in single-occupancy cells. In fact, when it was dedicated in 1912, it was the largest concrete structure in the world. To construct a building this size with adequate security measures, Turner conceived of the concept of double incarceration—that is, a prison within a prison. The outer prison, or cellhouse, consisted of the actual building with its massive eighteen-inch-thick concrete walls penetrated by windows that would later be covered with steel bars. Within this cellhouse were six cell blocks containing the six hundred actual cells. Each cell, block was designed in the shape of an "I" with two rows of cells, each three tiers high. A concrete walkway separated each cell block from the others and also from the exterior walls of the cellhouse, making each one into an island. To escape from Turner's prison within a prison, an inmate first had to escape from his cell, and then from the cellhouse. In the unlikely event that this double escape should occur, the escapee then would have to negotiate the waters of the bay before reaching land. No one thought this possible.

The construction of the administrative section, on the southern end of the cellhouse.

West side

The west side of the main cellhouse halfway through completion. The cellhouse at the time of its dedication was the largest concrete structure in the world.

The six cell blocks occupied the central and largest section of the cellhouse, an area 225 by 175 feet. The two cell blocks across from the corridors along the north and south walls of the cellhouse were the largest of the six, containing 126 cells each, while the four in between these two contained the remaining 348. All six cell blocks were three tiers high with eight iron spiral staircases providing access to the upper two tiers. Skylights set in the ceiling, a relatively new design, provided adequate light for all of the cell blocks during the day.

The cells in each of the six cell blocks were a comparatively spacious five by nine feet, more than double the size of the cells in the older wooden cellhouses. Within this confined space each prisoner was provided a steel spring cot suspended from one wall by chains, a chair, a ceiling light, and a small folding table at the opposite wall. A small sink with hot- and cold-water taps, along with a toilet, met the prisoner's personal hygienic needs.

PRISONER AUXILIARY ROOMS

Turner designated the north end of the cellhouse as the place for prisoner auxiliary rooms. Within this section of the cellhouse, Turner placed the mess hall, medical facility, showers, and storage. In placing these rooms within the cellhouse, he maintained tight security over the prisoners by eliminating the need for prisoners to leave the locked building.

The favorite room for the prisoners would be the mess hall. Sixty-four by thirty feet, this area was subdivided into several smaller rooms. The actual dining area where prisoners ate was thirty feet by forty feet and was the largest and most carefully guarded room in the prison. The adjacent kitchen, eighteen feet by thirty feet, was large enough for eight to ten prisoners to work in preparing food for the rest of the inmates. Separated from the mess hall by a large glass panel was a small mess hall for guards, who ate while keeping an eye on the prisoners

Two tiers of completed cells are shown. The framework for the third tier is in progress.

through the glass. The guards ate the same meals as the prisoners did, for which they paid ten cents for breakfast and lunch and fifteen cents for dinner.

The need to move large amounts of food into the kitchen area, which was located on the second floor, required a secure storage and preparation room on the first floor. To maintain tight security between the two floors, a single windowless stairway connected the two floors. Beneath the kitchen, cooks baked bread in an oven with a capacity of five hundred pounds of dough. During the later years of the prison, this room also was equipped with a two-ton compressor to provide refrigeration for stored food, an ice cream freezer, and an icemaker with a one-thousand-pound per day capacity. Although escape was unlikely, former inmates report that down here, removed from the constant surveillance of guards, bakers hid pots of fermenting

The mess hall and kitchen under construction. When completed, it would be the most carefully guarded area in the prison.

The Alcatraz medical staff in 1918. The black soldier in the second row was a former in-mate who regained soldier status and became an anesthetist in the prison hospital.

yeast to which they added various fruits to make homemade beer for their exclusive enjoyment.

Showers were required of all inmates once a week, except food handlers, who showered three times a week. Just as was the case in the mess hall and in the yard, bringing a large number of inmates together at the same time was considered risky by prison officials. Built in the basement of the north wing of the cellhouse, the shower room was fifty-five by twenty-five feet, intentionally small to accommodate only twenty-nine men at a time. The shower facilities were available to the inmates, one side of one cellblock tier at a time. Next to the showers, a barbershop was located; the inmates were required to get a regulation haircut every three weeks.

Shaving was a more complicated undertaking because razor blades were highly prized as weapons. Prisoners were allowed to shave three times a week. Each inmate had his own shaving mug, brush, and soap. Guards distributed razor blades to fifty prisoners at a time. Guards allowed fifteen minutes to shave after which they collected the blades. The blades were counted

An aerial view of the administration building, new lighthouse, and the warden's personal residence.

and when all were accounted for, they were given to the next fifty prisoners.

The infirmary, sixty feet by thirty feet, was little more than an elaborate first aid station. Seriously ill or injured inmates were either sent to San Francisco hospitals for short-term treatment or transferred to another federal penitentiary where long-term treatment was available. Each morning after head count, prisoners could see a medical assistant if they needed to.

The medical facility was isolated from the rest of the cellhouse on the north wing of the second floor. Access to it was by a stairwell that was equipped with a barred gate. Although the hospital was essentially one large ward, tight security was maintained at all times by dividing the ward into smaller sections with floor-to-ceiling bars. For reasons of health and security, inmates could receive only nonprescription medications and treatment for minor wounds.

A NEW LIGHTHOUSE

Although Alcatraz's function had changed from fort to prison, the island retained one historic role: keeping ships safe. In 1909 army engineers tore down the original lighthouse to make way for the construction of the new cellhouse. They replaced it with an eighty-four-foot-tall lighthouse constructed of steel and reinforced concrete and located next to the new cellhouse. At that height, the new lighthouse towered above the new three-story cellhouse to project its beam out to sea. Constructed at a cost of $35,000, the light from its lens reached nineteen miles out to sea beyond the Golden Gate.

The lens in the new lighthouse was the same third-order Fresnel from the original lighthouse. Surrounding the glass enclosure of the lens was a walkway called the lantern that was built to give the lighthouse keeper access in order to clean the glass. Each lighthouse had a distinct arrangement of its lenses, which allowed sailors far out to sea to identify the unique beam pattern of each lighthouse. The Alcatraz lighthouse's set of crystal prisms included two opposing bull's-eye lenses that magnified the light. As the lens rotated once every thirty seconds, it created the familiar flash each time a bull's-eye swung past the viewer's line of sight.

By the beginning of the 1930s, Alcatraz had the look and feel of a full-blown penitentiary. The army, however, was in the business of defending America from foreign enemies, not imprisoning its own soldiers. Besides, Alcatraz had ceased to be a strategic location and the extraordinarily high cost of maintenance caught budget planners' attention. The incessant pounding of salt air forced constant repair to buildings and the costs of ferrying supplies to the island were beginning to be a budgetary drain that would only get worse. And American social ills would soon create the demand for a slightly different use for Alcatraz.

Federal Maximum-
Security Prison

In 1934 the country had been reeling for several years under a crime wave linked to the historical era called Prohibition. In 1920, the Eighteenth Amendment to the U.S. Constitution had prohibited the production and sale of alcoholic beverages. Many Americans refused to give up alcohol, however, and during the 1920s criminal gangs in many of America's cities found an extremely lucrative business illegally supplying alcohol to the public. Accompanying the illegal sale of alcohol was a sharp rise in gang violence. The 1920s, in fact, became synonymous with high-profile gangsters creating havoc by engaging in alcohol smuggling, kidnapping, racketeering, and murder. Attorney General Homer Cummings was desperate to put a stop to these crimes.

In July 1933, J. Edgar Hoover, the director of the Federal Bureau of Investigation, decided to crack down on organized crime. Hoover focused on the most notorious of the gang bosses. The problem he faced was that, although the FBI caught these mob bosses and courts convicted them, corruption and lax prison regulations allowed them to continue their criminal activities from within prison walls. When Hoover heard that the army was thinking of giving up Alcatraz, he saw it as just what he had in mind as a location for a new federal penitentiary. With a maximum-security prison that was inaccessible and escape-proof, Hoover believed he could put the most notorious crime bosses out of business. Secondarily, he believed that the prospect of a life sentence on Alcatraz would serve as a deterrent to others who might be thinking of a life of crime.

PROHIBITION

Prohibition was the period of American history, from January 1920 to December 1933, during which time the federal government banned the manufacture and sale of alcohol. The near-total prohibition on alcohol was the result of many years of debate in the Congress and across America over the devastating effects of alcohol on people's health and family unity. The view expressed by the majority of Americans was that the elimination of alcohol would strengthen American citizens, their families, and the moral fiber of the country.

The period of Prohibition initiated a crime wave based on the illegal manufacture, distribution, and consumption of alcohol. The demand for alcohol stimulated the smuggling of alcohol in most major metropolitan areas where organized criminal gangs made millions of dollars selling the illegal booze. These gangs fought bloody wars with each other for the control of illegal alcohol distribution.

As more and more money flowed into the accounts of a few powerful criminals, their illegal activities spread beyond alcohol to drug distribution, illegal gambling, racketeering, kidnapping, and murder. Many large cities seemed helpless to stop the growth of gang activities, forcing the director of the FBI, J. Edgar Hoover, to declare war on these mobsters.

Hoover began placing the most powerful gang leaders and their cohorts on the FBI's list of the Ten Most Wanted criminals. Many captured crime bosses were incarcerated on Alcatraz because Hoover viewed them as incorrigible, and he wished to isolate them to prevent any further involvement in criminal activities. Many of the most infamous inmates at Alcatraz were involved at one time or another with violation of the laws governing Prohibition.

Twice during the early twentieth century, the army had seriously considered closing the military prison for financial reasons. When the army again expressed its interest in abandoning the island, the secretary of war, George Dern, asked Cummings if the Justice Department was interested in taking custody of the island and the prison. An agreement was struck, and on July 1, 1934, the attorney general turned custodianship of Alcatraz over to the federal Bureau of Prisons, ending the army's eighty-seven-year stewardship of the island.

Cummings knew that Alcatraz would by no means be self-sufficient, dependent as it was on ships to provide for all of the needs of staff and inmates. Food would come by boat from San Francisco's wharf, while special barges would bring fresh drinking water. An oil barge would be used to carry oil for the generators and gas for the trucks. Passenger boats would ferry people and mail from the Fort Mason pier. The children of the guards would have to be transported back and forth daily across the bay to attend San Francisco schools.

In spite of these many logistical obstacles, the next step for Cummings and Hoover was to convince the citizens of San Francisco that a maximum-security prison on Alcatraz would be a safe and prudent use of the island.

PUBLIC RESISTANCE

Many San Francisco organizations learned of the proposed handover and expressed their opposition to locating a maximum-security penitentiary so close to a major urban

J. Edgar Hoover, director of the FBI, declared war on the gangs that controlled smuggling of alcohol during Prohibition.

population. San Francisco's leading daily newspaper, the *Chronicle*, argued the potential for escapees' finding their way to San Francisco. The paper cited the fact that over the years, several military convicts had stolen boats and rowed to shore when Alcatraz was a military prison. Others had successfully forged release papers and were mistakenly released.

The Federation of Women joined the fray. Two young women members, Doris McCleod and Gloria Scigliano, doubt-

THE SEALED RAILROAD CARS OF AUGUST 22, 1934

When Alcatraz opened as a federal prison in 1934, thirty-two prisoners from the military prison were the first to occupy the federal maximum-security prison. Because J. Edgar Hoover, the director of the FBI, had designated Alcatraz as a maximum-security facility to control the most hardened criminals, he was eager to transfer many of America's most dangerous felons there. Toward this end, Hoover arranged to ship fifty-three carefully selected prisoners from penitentiaries in Lewisburg, Pennsylvania, and Atlanta, Georgia, to Alcatraz.

As guards unloaded the prisoners, they shackled them together in a long single chain and marched them up the road to the top of the island as guards armed with machine guns tracked every step from their vantage points on the watchtowers. Wives and children peered out their windows to watch notorious killers passing the officer housing on their way up the hill, mindful of warnings to remain indoors until guards had secured the celebrities. John Martini confides in his book, *Fortress Alcatraz*, that "One teenager nudged her mother and pointed to a stocky man with a pronounced double chin, midway in the chain of prisoners. 'There he is Mama! That's Al Capone!'"

ing that the 1.5-mile watery barrier was an adequate obstacle to escape, successfully swam out to the island to prove their point. The San Francisco school district raised concerns for the safety of schoolchildren should an escapee reach the city. San Francisco's chief of police, William J. Quinn, responded to the fears of residents living along the wharf by expressing concerns for the safety of its citizens if convicted murders should swim to shore and invade homes in the Marina District west of the wharf.

There was the additional fear that many of the gangsters slated for confinement on Alcatraz would extend their influence to criminal activities in San Francisco. In addition to citizens' concerns for safety, some also expressed the view that punishing offenders in maximum-security prisons without rehabilitating them was an immoral policy that ought not be pursued on Alcatraz.

In October 1933, the Justice Department released a statement stressing the security of the island. Spokesmen attempted to reassure all residents of San Francisco that renovations would raise Alcatraz to the level of a maximum-security prison that would eliminate any possibility of escape. In spite of the spirited opposition, the Justice Department moved forward with its plans to incarcerate the worst prisoners in the federal penitentiary system on Alcatraz. In a tersely worded statement issued on November 6, 1933, the Department of Justice responded to the concerns of the citizens of San Francisco:

> In brief, it seems to the Department of Justice that there is presented a splendid opportunity for the citizens of San Francisco to cooperate in a patriotic and public spirited manner in the Government's campaign against the criminal. The Department of Justice, while recognizing that civic pride and an interest in their community has prompted many of the recent communications which have come to the Department, nevertheless, bespeaks the cooperation and aid of this great community in the carrying on of this important and necessary activity.[8]

DESPERATE OR IRREDEEMABLE TYPES

To oversee the new federal maximum-security prison, James Bennett, the director of the Bureau of Prisons, and Hoover appointed James A. Johnston as the first warden. In overseeing this most unforgiving of penitentiaries, Johnston combined strict discipline with a zeal for progressive reform. Johnston, a onetime local banker, had been warden of the maximum-security San Quentin and Folsom prisons, both administered by the state of California. Johnston promised the Justice Department that the "confirmed criminals" of Alcatraz would not be allowed to commit more crimes and that nothing would be done to coddle them. To those convened for a special "crime clinic" in Washington, the warden said:

> Insistence on absolute obedience to regulations and the orders of those in authority is essential. I would not make a fetish of rules. I prefer reason. But there are rules of reason and reasonable rules, and prisoners should be

compelled to obey them; otherwise no progress can be made toward reformation, because chief of the criminal's faults is disobedience.[9]

Despite these moderate-sounding words, Johnston decided that the goal of Alcatraz was going to be not rehabilitation, but rather punishment for the inmate's life of crime. Federal prison officials were aware that modernization would be necessary to control the hardened criminals destined for Alcatraz. Controlling military deserters and petty thieves required only moderate security but under the new organization, the prison would house men whom Hoover referred to as desperate and irredeemable.

James A. Johnston, the first warden of Alcatraz. He was responsible for determining the goal of Alcatraz: to punish criminals rather than rehabilitate them.

In keeping with a policy of punishment, Johnston vowed that once the federal prison opened, he would ban access to newspapers, radios, and magazines. In addition, he decided that all incoming mail would be retyped by guards, so that coded messages contained in the original letters could not be received by the inmates. Johnston advocated a silence rule that would forbid inmates to speak with each other except in the recreation yard. Alcatraz was to be a limited-privilege prison as evidenced by rule number five of the Alcatraz regulations: "You are entitled to food, clothing, shelter, and medical attention. Anything else you get is a privilege."[10]

Cummings and Hoover, along with James Bennett, recognized that many repairs and improvements to the prison would be needed before the arrival of high-risk criminals. To that end, they hired Robert Bunge, a consulting engineer, to conduct a thorough assessment of the facilities and make recommendations to upgrade the military prison to a maximum-security prison.

One of Bunge's first recommendations was to drastically restrict prisoner access to other parts of the island to reduce the possibility of escape and to prevent the possibility of sabotage to

Inmates pass through metal detectors to prevent them from smuggling weapons into the cellhouse.

the electrical system and water supply. He knew that families of guards would be moving to the island and recommended that family housing be isolated from access by the prisoners. He recommended that the entire eastern side as well as other areas of the island be declared off-limits to prisoners. Several of the old tunnels used during the Civil War era as powder storage or as underground passageways Bunge ordered sealed with concrete or sealed at both ends by hardened steel gates.

Bunge recognized that prisoners would need access to a few limited areas such as the work buildings and the wharf. To prevent contraband from being moved around the island by prisoners, Bunge ordered the installation of metal detectors to aid in confiscation of objects that could be used as weapons or as tools for escape. Three metal detectors arrived on the island in 1934 and guards installed them at strategic locations. One was placed on the dock where all prisoners as well as visitors arrived, another at the entry to the cellhouse, and the third on the main road used by the prisoners to get to the work areas. Referred to as snitch boxes by the inmates, they reduced the presence of metal contraband within the prison population. To circumvent the snitch boxes, however, convicts learned to make weapons from brass, glass, and plastic, which the snitch boxes could not detect.

HARDENING THE CELL BLOCK

Bunge knew that the cellhouse would be a prime target for experienced criminals bent on escape. To match their ingenuity for finding escape routes, Bunge needed to harden the cellhouse. The six cell blocks within the cellhouse that had been built to accommodate six hundred prisoners when Alcatraz was a military prison were more than would be needed in the new maximum-security prison. Bunge therefore recommended the upgrade of the center four cell blocks of 348 cells and the deallocation of the remaining two outside cell blocks that then ran the length of the cellhouse next to the windows. These he ordered sealed off by steel mesh grates.

The primary focus of Bunge's recommendations, though, fell on the bars and doors of the cell blocks. The operation of cell doors in the old military prison necessitated the use of a unique key for each cell door, which required a large number of keys. Keys provided an additional security risk because to open and close the doors, a guard was always in close proximity to convicts. Bunge recommended that the federal prison upgrade security by installing a safer system for opening and closing cell doors.

To this end, federal prison officials hired the Stewart Baker Iron Works to build a mechanical system that guards could operate remotely, safely removed from the convicts. Installed in 1934, the new locking system allowed guards at one end of each cell block to open and close doors from a safe distance by remote control. This mechanical system was controlled by a series of steel levers housed behind locked doors located at the end of each cell block. The levers were connected to each cell door, allowing guards to open and close cell doors by lifting and lowering the levers. This mechanical system had the secondary benefit of allowing the guards to open one door at a time or a cluster of doors in unison. During the early years of the federal prison, when convicts were not allowed to speak to each other, the only noise convicts heard all day was the echoing metallic sound of the mechanical door system opening and slamming shut.

Tool-Proof Bars

The cell bars used in the old military prison were called flat bars because of their shape. Besides being flat, Bunge believed that the metal they were made

Each cell door was operated mechanically by remote control, eliminating the need for keys to every cell.

from was too soft for the new federal penitentiary. Although the old bars were made of iron, modern steel hacksaw blades could cut through them. In 1938, prison officials installed tool-proof bars, so named because the steel they were made from was especially hard and could resist the effects of cutting and drilling tools.

The bars actually were a laminated composite. The outer layer was steel and the inner core was tool-resistant carbon steel. The process that made the carbon steel tool-proof was the application of very high temperatures that hardened the crystal structure of the carbon steel. The composite bars were then laminated together by welding them along the length of the bar. The tool-proof bars were factory tested to ensure that they could withstand six hours of cutting by hacksaw blades and could resist being drilled by six 1/8-inch drill bits.

After tool-proof bars replaced the old flat bars on the cells, bars were also placed on all windows. Set so that they opened inward, the windows could let fresh air in but the bars on the outside prevented anyone from exiting. These tool-proof bar window coverings extended to all areas of inmate activities, including the hospital, library, and mess hall. All doors leading from one area of the cell block to another were also fitted with tool-proof bars. When all of the tool-proof work was completed, the cost of $216,927 exceeded the original cost of building the entire prison.

The designers developed tool-proof bars that could not be bent or cut.

Following the installation of the new tool-proof bars, prison officials carried out a series of their own tests to confirm the strength of the bars. Within one minute of the test, a hacksaw cut through the softer steel exterior layer of the bar but could not penetrate the case-hardened inner core. After dulling three hacksaw blades over a twenty-minute period, no deeper cut could be made.

The tool-proof bars did not stop the prison population from testing them from time to time, using smuggled hacksaw blades. When prisoners successfully made a cut into the soft exterior of a bar, they would blend the filings with paint to make a paste that could be smoothed over the cut to disguise the surface. Knowing this would happen, guards made unannounced tests of the bars with rubber mallets and learned to tell by the sound of the mallet striking the bar whether it had been cut.

Tool-proof bars added a great deal of security to the prison but they could not reduce the risk to guards who mingled among prisoners while escorting them to and from their cells and while they worked or exercised. To protect guards during times of close contact, prison designers added two additional security measures, gun galleries and guard towers.

GUN GALLERIES

The guards who walked the interior of the cell blocks, escorted prisoners to and from their cells, and supervised them outside of the cell blocks did so unarmed. This policy eliminated the risk of guards' losing their guns to prisoners in a scuffle. Guards placed themselves at risk but did so with the security of knowing that prison designers had taken precautions to protect them. To tighten security on the remaining four cell blocks, prison officials added two gun galleries at either end of the cell blocks extending from the second floor to the ceiling. Elevated off the ground to prevent prisoner access, these two gun galleries gave guards a view down and along the entire length of the cells. This was one of the few places on the island where guards had immediate access to weapons. As the unarmed guards patrolled and mingled with the prisoner population, they did so knowing that their compatriots in the gun galleries could assist them at a moment's notice. Likewise, inmates knew that an attack on a guard could draw gunfire from an armed guard in the gun gallery.

Solid steel plate covered the lower four feet of the galleries, with tool-proof bars running the rest of the way to the ceiling. These cages separated the gun galleries from the cell blocks. The stairs to the gun galleries were accessed through a steel door that was locked at all times and could be unlocked only by guards inside or by use of specially manufactured keys that were secured in locked control rooms. As guards monitored the movement of inmates, they remained behind steel bars through which they could shoot their weapons if necessary. From the gun galleries, guards had unobstructed fire lines throughout the walkways along the length of the cell blocks.

In the event that a guard's life was in danger, guards in the gun galleries had at their disposal a wide array of weaponry. Rather than place tear gas canisters on the walls of the cell blocks, prison officials opted to keep them in the gun gallery where guards could lob them down on rioting prisoners. In case a single prisoner attacked a guard, the gun gallery guards could discharge their handguns or carbine rifles for accurate pinpoint fire. In especially volatile and violent circumstances, they had Thompson submachine guns at their disposal.

Although highly effective, even the gun galleries were potentially vulnerable. For example, in the famous blast-out of

"Broadway," as it was known by both prisoners and guards, ran the length of the cellhouse.

1946, an inmate who had intentionally lost a great deal of weight was able to squeeze between two bars with the assistance of a bar spreader and gain access to the gun gallery, with disasterous results.

The gun galleries, the designers knew, would allow considerable control over the inmates within the prison but not during those times when they were outside the cellhouse. To extend close control over the areas outside of the cellhouse, prison officials implemented elaborate external security measures.

CONTROLLING THE PERIMETER

The motive for using Alcatraz as a maximum-security prison focused almost exclusively on the fact that, as an island, it isolated the inmates from the general population of the area. The swift-moving water surrounding the island provided an additional security barrier should prisoners escape from their cells. Because strong tidal currents were known to have pulled unlucky swimmers and boaters out to sea, authorities believed that escape from Alcatraz by swimming was impossible. Prison officials nonetheless were aware that access to the bay would be the goal of escapees, so they took several precautions to keep inmates away from the island's perimeter cliffs and isolated landings.

In 1934 the Anchor Post Fence Company installed cyclone fencing topped with barbed wire around most of the perimeter of the island. The fence created both a barrier to the bay as well as a barrier excluding inmates from the many auxiliary buildings on the island.

Out of concern that some of the inmates might have friends on the outside who might try to use a boat to pick up an escapee, efforts were made to keep all watercraft away from the island. Bureau of Prison regulations stipulated that the many pleasure craft plying the waters of the San Francisco Bay maintain a 300-yard distance from the island. Local yachtsmen were familiar with the eighteen-by-twenty-foot sign:

WARNING
KEEP OFF
ONLY GOVERNMENT BOATS PERMITTED
WITHIN 300 YARDS OF ALCATRAZ.
PERSONS ATTEMPTING TO ENTER
WITHOUT AUTHORITY DO SO AT THEIR PERIL.

ALCATRAZ GOES TO WAR

The Japanese attack on Pearl Harbor on December 7, 1941, followed by America's declaration of war, reminded Americans of the strategic importance of Alcatraz. Driven by fears of a possible Japanese air attack on San Francisco, the military initiated discussions with prison officials to arm Alcatraz with large weapons.

Military strategists reasoned that if the Japanese attacked by air, the location of Alcatraz in the middle of the bay would be a perfect place from which to shoot down the attacking planes. With that objective in mind, three 37-mm antiaircraft guns arrived on the island along with army crews trained to fire them. The highest location on the island to place the guns was on top of the main cellblock, 150 feet above the water. Mounted high above the other buildings, gunners had an unobstructed view of San Francisco and the cities of Berkeley and Oakland on the east side of the bay.

The early irony of the antiaircraft guns was that the crews ferried to the island in the morning and returned at night. If an attack had come during the day, the crews would have responded, but if an attack had occurred at night, no one would have been there to defend the island or

At the Alcatraz wharf an eight-foot-square sign further warned:

UNITED STATES
PENITENTIARY
ALCATRAZ ISLAND—AREA 12 ACRES
1½ MILES TO TRANSPORT DOCK
ONLY GOVERNMENT BOATS PERMITTED.
OTHERS MUST KEEP OFF 300 YARDS.
NO ONE ALLOWED ASHORE
WITHOUT A PASS.

Although the actual area of the island was twenty-two acres, no one argued when a guard using the loudspeaker initially admonished those who ignored the warning signs. Failure to heed his call drew warning shots from the guards occupying the guard towers. These measures were effective: No escape at-

San Francisco. Barracks on Alcatraz later housed the crews which, although welcomed, were not openly accepted by the prison staff.

During the course of World War II, no Japanese attack occurred, although Japanese submarines operated off the California coast. Although the antiaircraft crews drilled regularly, they never fired their guns with live ammunition. This unusual circumstance led many convicts to believe that the guns were merely scale models incapable of firing real ammunition.

During practice air raid drills, many prisoners hid under their steel spring bunks hysterically crying, knowing that if bombs actually struck the cellblock, none would escape alive. Near the end of the war, the army removed the antiaircraft guns and peacetime monotony replaced wartime monotony.

A 37-mm antiaircraft gun being hoisted to the top of the guards' apartment house. Two other guns were placed on the prison roof for use in case of a Japanese air raid during World War II.

tempt ever involved the landing of a craft on the island with the intent of assisting an escape. In fact, the only recorded unauthorized landing was by a stern-wheeler named the *Delta King,* which crashed off the southeast tip of the island. The Coast Guard dispatched a cutter to assist the boat off the rocks.

Surveillance of the outside of the prison was an important part of the enhanced security measures. The transition from military prison to federal prison also brought the addition of four guard towers, sometimes called machine-gun towers. These towers served as a constant reminder to the inmates that even when they were outside the prison, they were being watched at all times. Two more towers were added in 1936, for a total of six strategically placed to ring the island. Heavily armed guards high above the prison buildings watched the movement of inmates while they were outside of the cellhouse, to ensure that

Supplies for the prison are unloaded and sent through a metal detector. Almost everything prisoners or guards needed on the island had to be brought by boat from San Francisco.

none attempted to work their way to the bay. Some built of wood and others of steel, the towers housed one guard at a time in an hexagonal kiosk high off the ground.

The dark of night compounded the difficulties for officers assigned to the guard towers. At night large searchlights assisted guards as the light swept the roofs of the buildings and the perimeter of the island. Watchful guards relied on sound to discern unusual movement below them. To be effective, guards learned to distinguish the natural sounds of waves breaking on the shore, barking of sea lions, and bird cries from those of human movement.

On many occasions, guards stationed in the towers opened fire on inmates, warned off approaching boats with their bullhorns or guns, and assisted guards on the ground in searching for missing prisoners.

The guards and prisoners played a cat-and-mouse game with deadly seriousness. Every decision made by the warden and his staff took into consideration the safety of both the guards and prisoners. The key to a well-run penal institution was to create a physical and psychological environment where both groups of men could coexist safely.

Guard towers such as this one were manned twenty-four hours a day to watch for any escape attempts.

KEEPING INMATES AND THEIR GUARDS SECURE

The most difficult and most dangerous task of running a maximum-security prison was providing for the safety of the prisoners and guards. Leading very different lives on opposite sides of the law, both guards and prisoners lived and worked at close quarters in a potentially explosive environment. Maintaining safe surroundings for these two groups was a constant challenge for the warden and his staff. From the moment prisoners first set foot on Alcatraz to the day they departed, policies and procedures governed every minute of their lives and every movement they made. Much of the structure of the prison was designed to give guards maximum control over their charges. In addition, much of what went on at the prison—initially at least—was kept from the public.

The first arrival of federal prisoners on Alcatraz occurred cloaked in secrecy and intrigue. The director of the FBI, J. Edgar Hoover, carefully picked this first group of prisoners from among the most dangerous and notorious of inmates already housed in other federal prisons throughout the United States. Isolating them on Alcatraz island, Hoover speculated, would not only isolate them from the general prison population but would also prevent them from continuing to control their criminal organizations from their cells. Nevertheless, prisoners still needed some optimism that they might someday earn their release. Without that sense of optimism, Warden Johnston knew they might try to escape, or worse, assault guards or other inmates.

Warden Johnston and FBI Director Hoover shared the view that the purpose of Alcatraz was to punish the inmates, not to rehabilitate them. In spite of the simplicity of this harsh view,

ROBERT "BIRDMAN" STROUD

The island's most famous prisoner, Robert Stroud (594-AZ), the so-called Birdman of Alcatraz, in reality never had any birds at Alcatraz. As a maximum-security prison, Alcatraz did not permit guards to extend to inmates special privileges such as raising birds. Stroud's fame as the Birdman of Alcatraz resulted from a fictitious film treatment of his life, in which Burt Lancaster portrayed Stroud with his birds as his cellmates. Far from being the kindly grandfather figure in the movie, guards who knew Stroud considered him one of the most vicious psychopaths in the history of the prison.

Robert Stroud, the famous "Birdman" of Alcatraz. He was regarded as one of the island's most dangerous and unstable inmates.

In 1909, Stroud committed his first murder, for which he was sentenced to a federal prison for twelve years. After three years, prison officials transferred Stroud to Leavenworth federal prison, where he viciously attacked and murdered a guard in the mess hall while two thousand fellow prisoners watched. Although he received the death sentence, President Woodrow Wilson commuted the sentence to life imprisonment.

During his stay at Leavenworth, he developed his interest in birds and eventually wrote two books about canaries and their diseases. Initially, prison officials allowed Stroud to study canaries, believing it to be therapeutic. In time, however, guards ordered his transfer to Alcatraz in 1942 when they discovered that Stroud was using his birds and bird-related equipment to smuggle alcohol.

While at Alcatraz, Stroud's vicious character caused him to be sent to solitary confinement for six of his seventeen years, the most of any inmate. In 1959, he died in the medical center for federal prisoners in Springfield, Missouri.

Johnston's task of containing and controlling prisoners was a daunting one. A key to his success would be delicately balancing his need for security with their need to hope for a better future. Toward this end, Warden Johnston directed the daily activities of operating Alcatraz.

A Prisoner's First Day

Moving hardened criminals to Alcatraz who knew that they had little to lose presented special problems. Traveling outside of the walls of any prison presented inmates with an obvious opportunity for escape. Prison officials knew that this problem could become even more complicated if associates and family members of the prisoners being transported knew of their movements and tried to free them. This was particularly true of the new inhabitants of Alcatraz, many of whom were men with long histories of violent behavior and well-organized friends who would willingly commit additional crimes in the process of freeing them.

On August 11, 1934, a train arrived in nearby Oakland carrying the first fourteen federal prisoners from McNeil Island penitentiary in the state of Washington. From Oakland, a prison boat carried them to the dock at the Alcatraz wharf. Guards armed with machine guns signed off on their arrival. Secrecy was of paramount importance to deter those who might try to rescue them. All telegram transmissions between Warden Johnston and James Bennett, director of the Bureau of Prisons, were coded. Upon the arrival of the first fourteen prisoners, Johnston sent the following telegram to his superiors in Washington: "Fourteen crates furniture arrived from McNeil received in good condition. Now installed."[11] The first shipment went well; Johnston and Bennett confidently awaited the next group, which included some of the toughest inmates in the federal prison system.

To minimize the risk of transporting some of the toughest criminals in America, FBI director Hoover took no chances. He decided to transfer them in three sealed railroad cars. Guards sealed the cars by welding steel bars over the windows and padlocking the doors to ensure that no one could escape during train stops. Within the three cars, the prisoners remained handcuffed and chained together at the ankles.

The FBI tried to conceal the transfer of these infamous prisoners from the press but somehow news of the event leaked out and reporters were waiting for the train in Oakland, on the east

GEORGE "MACHINE GUN" KELLY

George "Machine Gun" Kelly (117-AZ) became a household name across much of America in the 1930s as a brazen bank robber, kidnapper, and killer. Born George Kelly Barnes in Memphis, Tennessee, July 18, 1895, he was the son of an insurance executive, and grew up in a well-to-do family that provided him with a good education, including college.

Kelly was rumored to be capable of firing his "chopper" so accurately that he could write his name on a piece of wood in lead. There may have been some truth to his proficiency because the FBI wanted poster on Kelly, dated August 14, 1933, describes him as an expert machine gunner.

The press and public knew Kelly best for his many kidnappings of wealthy people, most famously of millionaire Charles F. Urschel, a crime for which the FBI arrested Kelly and his gang members. Kelly arrived on Alcatraz on the sealed train of 1934 along with Al Capone. A former guard at Alcatraz, Frank Heaney, remembers Kelly this way in his book, *Inside the Walls of Alcatraz:*

George "Machine Gun" Kelly

> Kelly served as the altar boy at the Catholic services, and also as the projectionist for the movies. He was somewhat shy at first with those he didn't know, but after a while he tended to warm up; and he did to me probably because both of us were Irish. He really was a nice fellow, and reminded me more of a bank president than a bank robber. As far as I could tell, he was one of the most stable prisoners on the island.

Kelly was sent to Leavenworth prison in 1951 after suffering a heart attack. He was paroled in early 1954 and died a few months later of a heart attack on July 18, 1954, his fifty-ninth birthday.

This sealed train car contained some of the most infamous inmates who would call Alcatraz home, including Al Capone and George Kelly.

shore of San Francisco Bay. The FBI learned that the press would be on hand so they detoured the train to the small city of Tiburon on the north shore of the bay. As an absolute guarantee that this load of prisoners would not have the opportunity to escape, a barge built to handle railroad cars was rented and the three sealed cars were pulled onto the barge. On August 22, 1934, a tugboat towing the barge loaded with the three sealed train cars and their fifty-three passengers docked at the Alcatraz wharf.

Guards armed with machine guns unlocked the padlocks on the train doors and signed off on their arrival. Newly hired federal guards, nervous about the simultaneous arrival of many of the most notorious criminals in America, shackled them together in a long chain gang. Guards then marched the disheveled convicts past the newly constructed guard tower, through the sally port, and up the winding road, and delivered them to Johnston for first-day processing. This process became the routine for all subsequent arrivals on Alcatraz.

Processing new prisoners entailed a series of interrogations that would determine what cell each would be assigned and any

AL "SCARFACE" CAPONE

Without a doubt the most notorious inmate to serve time on Alcatraz, Al Capone (85-AZ) led a rather quiet existence during his four and a half years on the Rock. Capone's criminal reputation as a gangland killer originated during Prohibition.

One of the effects of Prohibition was a dramatic increase in organized crime associated with the illegal sale of alcohol. Much of the crime occurring in large eastern cities was organized around gangs that controlled alcohol as well as many other illegal activities. Capone led one of these organizations. Known as Scarface because of a knife cut to his cheek, Capone was born in Naples, Italy, and raised in Brooklyn, New York, but concentrated his criminal activites in Chicago.

Al "Scarface" Capone was easily the most notorious of all the inmates ever to stay on Alcatraz.

After many years of illegal activities, a jury finally convicted Capone of income tax evasion in 1931 and he was sentenced to eleven years in prison. In 1934 he arrived at Alcatraz on the infamous sealed railroad car carrying some of the first federal prisoners. Despite his fame, Capone was just another inmate who received neither special privileges nor the respect of the other inmates. Capone first worked in the prison laundry and later cleaning the showers. Although once stabbed in a fight and once placed in solitary confinement for eight days because of another fight, Capone maintained a fairly low profile. Capone spent most of his time in the prison's hospital suffering from syphilis that caused brain degeneration.

Capone became increasingly debilitated, and after spending long periods of time in the prison hospital, Alcatraz officials paroled him in 1939 to his home in Florida, where he died in 1947.

SARGE

During World War II, John Giles, an inmate working on the dock, painstakingly assembled a sergeant's uniform one piece at a time. With help from friends working in the laundry rooms, Giles slowly pilfered sleeves, a collar, buttons, zippers, and even a hat. When he had completed his uniform, he put it on under his prison overalls, then watched for his chance, stripped off his prisoner's uniform, and hopped aboard a boat returning to shore. Not realizing that the guards on the boat counted the men on the way over, he thought he was a free man as the boat headed back. Unbeknownst to him, however, the ship's captain radioed back to Alcatraz that one too many men was on the boat. The captain of the guard on Alcatraz grabbed a fast launch and arrived on the dock ahead of the ferry. As Giles, disguised as a sergeant, stepped off the ferry, his face fell when he saw the grinning captain of the guard waiting for him with handcuffs.

Giles came closer to escaping than any other federal convict. The other inmates nicknamed him "Sarge" and he lost his work privileges for one year, after which he was assigned the worst job on the island, running the incinerator.

special needs each might have. Guards admitted all inmates through the rear of the prison and took them directly to the shower facilities, where their clothes were taken from them. Medical officers then searched them for drugs or weapons hidden in body cavities. Following this thorough strip search, guards issued each man his Alcatraz name and number card, which the guards referred to as the "name and number ticket." The official number assigned to each inmate consisted of the assigned digits followed by the AZ designation unique to Alcatraz. Gangster Al Capone, for example, was assigned 85-AZ.

Once prisoners had showered and undergone thorough physical checkups, correctional officers made decisions about where to house each new arrival, so as to separate potentially violent inmates or to separate men who were members of the same gang. Decisions were also made regarding how an inmate would spend any time outside of his cell. If the guards determined the prisoner to be trustworthy, they granted him the privilege of working in the shop industries building on the northwest corner of the island. There he would labor making uniforms or cleaning prison laundry. At his cell, each inmate received a copy of the rules and regulations, which he signed and was expected to learn.

THE CELL

At the heart of the entire prison system were the cells separating inmates from each other and from the guards. Without question, prisoners spent more time here than any other place on Alcatraz. Depending on their trustworthiness, inmates spent from fifteen to twenty-three hours a day in their cells. In one way, a cell on Alcatraz was relatively luxurious. Five by nine feet in size, it was larger than those used when Alcatraz was a military prison. And unlike the practice in most federal prisons, inmates did not share the cells with other prisoners. The front of the cell, half barred door and half stationary bars, provided the prisoner's only view of his surroundings. For most it was a view across the central corridor into the cells of other prisoners.

As was true of the rest of the prison, the cells were constructed to minimize the opportunity for escape. Three walls of the cell were made of solid concrete rather than cement block because solid concrete walls are stronger and harder to tunnel through. In particular, the designers of the prison were concerned with the back wall of the cell be-

This utility corridor was located behind the back wall of the cells.

cause behind it, there was located a utility corridor containing all of the water pipes running to the cells and the larger wastewater lines coming from them. This corridor had to be wide enough to allow workers access to the water and waste lines and therefore was also wide enough for an escaped prisoner to move through. If convicts managed to gain access to this corridor, shinnying up the pipes to the roof and then to freedom was a possibility.

When the prison's designers modernized the cell block for use as a federal prison, they modernized the heating system and added air ducts for better circulation of air. To carry fresh air to each cell, the air ducts ran from the roof down and along the utility corridor and finally through a steel grate into each cell. This steel grate was directly set into the concrete to prevent its removal and its size was intentionally small enough to discourage anyone from thinking he could squeeze through it.

Even though the cells were small, storage areas were designed with security in mind. The two storage shelves were set in clear view across the back wall and prisoners were responsible for placing all personal items in the correct place as specified by a diagram in the *Institution Rules & Regulations*. This policy allowed guards to scan quickly a prisoner's cell and determine the presence of contraband. Each morning after rising, prisoners swept their cells, placing trash in a trash basket that was later collected for disposal, hauled down to the incinerator, and burned.

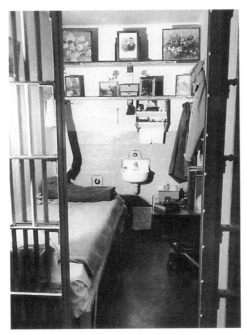

The typical Alcatraz cell was five feet by nine feet. Prisoners spent up to twenty-three hours a day in their cells.

Confinement in the cell blocks was generally sufficient punishment to keep the men under control. At times, however, some inmates became so abusive toward guards and fellow prisoners that additional restraints were necessary to control them. To this end, some inmates were isolated from the rest of the prison population in D-block.

D-BLOCK

Between the opening of the federal prison in 1934 and 1939, Johnston recognized the need for a cell block for inmates whose behavior warranted stricter discipline or punishment. For a few years before 1939, Johnston used the old abandoned Citadel underground basement, called the dungeon, to hold unruly inmates until their attitude improved. In 1939, however, bowing to public opinion that incarceration in the dungeon was cruel, Johnston ordered one of the old unused cell blocks converted for use as a place of special confinement. This special cell block had enough cells to accommodate forty-two prisoners.

The guards sent most men to D-block because of rule violations such as refusal to follow orders, hiding contraband in cells, fighting among prisoners, attempting an escape, and the worst violation of all, attacking a guard. Secondarily, inmates went there because of bad attitude. Frank Heaney, a guard on Alcatraz, explained D-block this way:

> The length of sentence to solitary was determined first of all by the seriousness of the incident that got you there, and secondly by your attitude once inside those cells. They were like special attitude adjustment cells. Typical bad attitude would be shown by spitting on us, throwing food, urine or feces at us, cursing us.[12]

D-block was divided into three distinct cell types: thirty-six normal cells called "isolation" by the inmates, five cells with solid sides that blocked sunlight, collectively called "the hole," and one called "the strip cell."

The thirty-six isolation cells were similar to the regular cells with steel bars on the front but were a bit larger because federal prisons were subject to new guidelines for cell size developed during a modernization program in 1940. The difference between life in these isolation cells and the regular cells was simply one of restricted movement. Prisoners here did not leave their cells to eat, work, or exercise. Isolation meant that they remained in their cells twenty-four hours a day. Guards brought meals to these cells, allowing the inmates only one hour a week for exercise and a ten-minute shower. Even the shower was isolated from the rest of the inmates.

These cells in D-block were used to isolate and punish inmates when they broke prison rules.

The five dark cells, the hole, were cell numbers nine through thirteen and were larger than the other cells, six feet three inches by twelve feet nine inches. Each of these five cells had a double door system. The inner door was the standard tool-proof bar door but there was also an outer door made of solid iron weighing two hundred pounds that blocked out all light and sound. The iron doors on these cells had peepholes through which guards could monitor a prisoner but total darkness was the prisoner's entire experience. These cells housed inmates who had committed major rule violations. The interior of these iron boxes had a sink and a toilet but the deprivation of light and sound had a devastating effect on the men who occupied them and most did not want to return. Regulations placed a nineteen-day limit on each stay in the hole.

The one strip cell, rarely used, was reserved for prisoners whose attitude had reached a point of uncontrollable belligerence toward the guards or other convicts. The intent for creating this most severe cell was to create an environment so unpleasant that inmates would never want to return.

The strip cell was one of the dark cells except it had neither a sink nor a toilet. Inside of this totally dark box was a hole in the floor that served as a toilet. Food consisted only of watery soup, bread, and water. At night, guards placed bedding in the cells but removed it in the morning. Offenders remained in total darkness, often without their clothes. Because of the severity of deprivation in this cell and the constant damp chill from lack of blankets and clothes, incarcerations were limited to three days.

THE MESS HALL

Life in D-block could be terrible; life even in the main cell blocks was hard enough. Mealtimes presented the few opportunities many inmates had to leave their cells. Security surrounding meals was more tightly observed than for any other activity because this was the only place where all inmates were together at one time. The potential for riot, violence, or even escape was always present. Three times a day, inmates filed into the mess hall for their meals. This concentration of the entire prisoner population in the mess area, except those in isolation, necessitated unusual security. Johnston was keenly aware of the potential for danger:

The mess hall was a dangerous place for inmates and guards. Tear gas canisters were attached to the ceiling and could be triggered by remote control in case of a riot.

It is impossible to predict what will happen or when or where but experience has shown that the mess hall is generally the place where agitators focus mass action.[13]

Johnston was correct in his concern for security in the mess hall. Once, for example, an irate prisoner knocked him unconscious during a meal. Following this incident, Johnston ordered the installation of fourteen tear gas canisters in the cafeteria and kitchen at the cost of $9,050. Bolted to the ceiling of the mess hall, the canisters could be triggered by remote control in case of a riot or other disturbance.

Even tighter security was needed in the kitchen that adjoined the mess hall because of the use of butcher knives to cut meats and vegetables for meals. The kitchen was the only area in the prison where prison officials permitted their use. Prisoners working with knives were separated from the other prisoners in the mess hall by concrete and glass walls to prevent knives from finding their way into the general prison population.

Prison guards controlled and monitored these knives more closely than any other tool on the island. The butcher knives were stored by hanging them on wood holders with the outline of each knife painted on the wood behind it. The painted outlines allowed the guards to know with a quick glance which knives were missing. Despite the precautions, during the history of Alcatraz, three inmates were killed in butcher knife stabbings and several more were wounded.

The prison staff also knew that the mess hall was one source of metal objects that inmates could craft into tools for escape or for use as weapons. Following each meal, guards collected and counted all forks, spoons, and metal juice pitchers before dismissing the inmates from the mess hall. The prisoners were highly resourceful, though, in getting around such measures. On more than one occasion guards found smuggled forks and spoons during their searches of cells.

Though prisoners received food through steel bars designed to keep them away from the kitchen knives, there were stabbing deaths at Alcatraz.

Visitors

Always fearing the worst, prison officials severely limited visitors to Alcatraz in an effort to reduce the possibility of escape and to prevent contraband from reaching inmates. Prison regulations restricted visitors to immediate family members and attorneys. Regulations permitted one family member to visit once a month between 1:30 P.M. and 3:10 P.M. Prisoners arranged visits with their attorneys through the office of the associate warden.

When a family member or attorney arrived, he or she was first searched. The searches that a visitor was subjected to were thorough to the point of being humiliating. Always on the lookout for contraband, guards subjected members of inmates' families to strip searches. A story is commonly

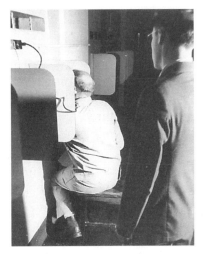

Visitors were separated from prisoners by glass in an attempt to keep contraband from being smuggled into the prison.

told about Al Capone's elderly mother, who, after undergoing the humiliation of a strip search, never again visited her son.

Following the search, guards led visitors to a room inside the cellhouse but separate from the cell blocks themselves. A bank of telephones in this room was connected through a concrete and glass partition to the inside of the cell block just below one of the gun galleries.

When a prisoner was notified of a visitor, he sat on the cell block side of the wall looking at the visitor through the window and speaking into a handset. To eliminate the passing of drugs, escape tools, or escape plans, no physical contact was allowed. Prison officials monitored all the phone conversations and could disconnect the phone call at any time if forbidden subjects were discussed. Any discussions about other inmates, buildings on the island, or prison security procedures would cause the guards to disconnect the phone lines.

The stark reality of the visitor policy was that most men never received a single visitor, with the exception of their lawyers. Most inmates did not have family in the San Francisco area and travel to Alcatraz for a one hour and forty minute visit was costly. Family members who did make the long trip usually arranged a two-day visit by scheduling time on the last day of one month and first day of the next month.

THE YARD

Lacking most freedoms, inmates tended to obey prison rules in order to keep their privileges of working and spending time in the exercise yard. Inmates considered the exercise yard to be the only place in the prison where they could choose their own activity. This large rectangular exercise area was located outside of the northwest corner of the cellhouse. Roughly 175 by 100 feet, the yard was constructed at the same time as the cellhouse during the early 1900s. To prevent inmates from escaping, engineers surrounded the yard with twenty-foot concrete walls topped with barbed wire. When Alcatraz became a federal prison, two iron cages were constructed at the tops of two of the corners of the yard from which armed guards could keep an eye on the activities of the inmates below.

Prisoners with a history of good behavior could spend a few hours a week in the yard doing whatever they liked. One end of the yard had a dirt baseball field where inmates played their favorite team sport. The corner of the yard closest to the cellhouse

The recreation yard was the only place on Alcatraz where prisoners were allowed the freedom to choose their own activities.

had a large flight of stairs leading up to the cell block. During the early 1900s, before Alcatraz was a federal prison, this area was an outcropping of heavy boulders. Engineers, fearful that desperate prisoners might use these boulders as weapons, removed them and built a broad flight of concrete stairs where men could sit and watch the baseball game, play cards, or talk with friends. Besides being the only place for exercise and talking with friends, the yard was the only place where inmates were able to get fresh air and occasional sun.

One of the tasks assigned to inmates at the outbreak of World War II was welding seams on a flotation buoy used to secure the anti-submarine net at the entrance to San Francisco Bay.

Prison officials were aware of the risks associated with allowing this many men to congregate in one place. To control the prisoners, access to the yard was restricted by two gates; one led from the cellhouse and the other gave access to a steep flight of stairs on the west side leading to work areas. To make surveillance of inmates simpler, at no time were both gates open at the same time. Given the large number of men congregated at one time, the yard was not always a safe place for the prisoners. Although guards in the yard mingled with the prisoners and at least one fully armed officer stood in the guard tower overlooking the area, violence occasionally broke out.

WORK

Time in the yard was one diversion; work was another. Work on Alcatraz was a privilege, not a requirement. Even the most belligerent inmates quickly learned that work was one of the few diversions from the never-ending boredom of highly regimented prison life. Those not trusted to work passed the entire day, except for meal times, in their locked cells.

Each day, following breakfast and the head count, inmates assigned to jobs lined up in the walled recreation yard. In long single file lines they walked down the steep steps to the industries building. The Prison Industries building, where most inmates worked, was a large two-story rectangular warehouselike building on the northwest corner of the island. Here men worked on the first floor repairing wood furniture and making prison uniforms, including shoes. During World War II, prisoners joined in the war effort by making cargo nets and rubber mats and repairing metal buoys that supported the antisubmarine net submerged at the entrance to San Francisco Bay. On the second floor, the prison operated the laundry for cleaning all of the prison uniforms as well as bedding and towels.

The Prison Industries building was also a place where many escape attempts began because of the availability of useful materials and tools. This was one of the few places on the island where men could scrounge pieces of metal that could be used as weapons, or tools like chisels and hacksaws, which could be used for escape. To control this problem, counts of tools were

An aerial view of Alcatraz shows the industry and shop areas.

made on a regular basis and all workers passed through a metal detector on their way back to the cellhouse before lunch and at the end of the day. In spite of these precautions, various pieces of metal and tools found their way to the cellhouse. Prisoners sometimes sneaked around the metal detectors when guards weren't looking.

Prison officials knew that the location of the industries building, outside the cellhouse, also gave men trying to escape direct access to the bay. To prevent escape, the windows of the industries building were fitted with tool-proof bars, guards escorted the inmates to and from the cellhouse, and head counts were conducted before and after entering and leaving the industries building.

Away from the industries building, a small number of inmates worked in other parts of the island. A dozen men worked in the kitchen preparing the thousand meals a day that inmates and guards consumed. Among the most coveted jobs was working as a runner to deliver library books to the inmates' cells and working on the wharf loading and unloading the supply ships. Prisoners new to Alcatraz might be able to work sweeping the cell block or cleaning up the recreation yard. After the first month, they were usually assigned to a more permanent position in the industries building.

The line between the prisoners and guards was sometimes thin, often blurred. Both were victims of the rules, regimentation, and regulations. The clock governed all of their lives and the walls restricted their movements. While at work, both guards and prisoners lived strikingly similar lives. While not at work however, the lives of the guards were very different. Working on the Rock while trying to maintain a normal family life, however, was a tricky matter.

GUARDS AND THEIR FAMILIES

Although the prison population was relatively small for a federal penitentiary, averaging about 260 men, the guard population was comparatively large. Technically known as correctional officers, the number of guards averaged 1 for every 5 inmates. The total count of all civilian workers on the island in 1935 stood at 2 administrative officers—warden and deputy warden—5 lieutenants, 49 guards, 1 chaplain, 23 clerical workers, and 8

Several guards stand ready to leave the prison when their shift is over. After work, guards could go to an entertainment hall reserved for their use.

mechanics. An inspector for the U.S. Treasury Department counted civilian heads in 1936 and reported 158 adults, including wives of guards, and 64 children. Alcatraz had enough inhabitants to qualify as a legitimate small town. Strange as it has always seemed for outsiders, the guards and their families went on with their lives in a remarkably normal manner.

NOT ONLY A PRISON BUT ALSO A COMMUNITY

In spite of the imposing structure of the cellhouse, machine-gun towers, and endless barbed wire, families on Alcatraz led surprisingly ordinary lives. Children grew up playing the same games as other children in thousands of American communities, wives followed daily domestic routines, and guards discharged their work responsibilities before going home to their families. Although the guards and their families lived within one of the most bizarre neighborhoods on earth, they nonetheless formed a tight community. Even to this day, the guards, all of whom are now retired, maintain contact with each other through a newsletter and an annual alumni dinner.

The vast majority of the time, families went about their lives disconnected and unconcerned with the presence of the prison population, but the rare exception was memorable. Mike Pitzer, the son of a guard, remembered his first escape experience when guards spotted an escaped convict clinging to a rock about one hundred yards off Alcatraz:

> Boy! They opened fire on the rock. . . . That was unreal. That was the first time I had been around a prison break where they did any shooting. . . . I went outside and [saw officers] up on the roof, and they were firing all kinds of shots. I thought they would blow the rock away. They even had two Coast Guard boats on the backside and [the prisoner] wouldn't give up. Then I remember the front guy [Coast Guard officer] holding him with a grappling hook and pulling him in.[14]

STAFF HOUSING

Housing the prison staff and their families required security precautions similar to those employed in the cellhouse. Of primary consideration was the separation of families from the inmate population. To this end, prison authorities isolated all family housing and family activities at the extreme southern end of the island. Although the island was small, a mere twenty-two acres, family housing and family activities were nonetheless located as far from the cellhouse and prisoner work areas as possible.

Chain-link fencing topped with barbed wire surrounded the family housing area. Access to this area was through a series of locked gates. Family members quickly adapted to the routine of unlocking gates to get home. Although no escaped convict ever entered the family housing area of the island, the gates were not necessarily what deterred them. One day one of the children playing with Popsicle® sticks was passing through a gate and discovered that he could

> unlock those locks with a Popsicle stick. You shoved a stick in there, twisted it and it opened the lock. I called [Guard] Miller or Madigan and said, "I think there is something you might be interested in. . . ." [He laughs.] I gave 'em a demonstration and about two days later all the locks were changed.[15]

The warden, the highest-ranking prison administrator, occupied the most impressive house on the island. Constructed in 1922, it originally housed the commander of the military prison. Built on the southern tip of the island, it commanded a panoramic view of San Francisco as well as an over-the-shoulder-glance to the north in the direction of the ominous-looking cellhouse. Designed to reflect the Spanish history of Alcatraz, its concrete exterior resembled adobe and the front façade featured bell towers common to the Spanish missions built in California during the eighteenth century. At the time the residence was constructed, mission revival architecture was a popular style and was widely used on military bases throughout California.

Built to function as the warden's residence as well as to reflect his importance, this house had fifteen rooms with amenities reflecting the warden's status. The rooms of the house were spacious and ornately decorated. The only fireplace on the island was used in a large reception room where dignitaries from the city of San Francisco as well as directors of the federal prison system were entertained. All four federal wardens who served on Alcatraz lived there.

As the highest-ranking officer, the warden was entitled to the largest house on the island, an ornately decorated, fifteen-room mansion.

A row of guards' residences on Alcatraz. These were rented out to correctional officers for a mere twenty-five dollars a month, including free laundry.

Living in San Francisco was not an option for most guards and their families because a guard's salary of $1,680 a year during the 1930s was not enough to rent a house, so the Bureau of Prisons made arrangements for living quarters on the island. The old barracks, built during the military prison era, were remodeled in 1934 into eleven multiroom apartments for families and nine single-room apartments for bachelors. In addition to these new units, an old building near the wharf was converted into twelve additional apartments. These apartments were rented to prison staff for a modest twenty-five dollars a month, and laundry service was thrown in free. In addition, guards were entitled to eat the same meals the convicts ate, for which they paid between ten and fifteen cents.

ENTERTAINMENT

Despite the benefits that came with the job, tensions often ran high in the cellhouse and many a veteran guard was eager for his two days off each week. One of their favorite places to relax was the Officers' Club, the building that had served as the post exchange during the military years. Located near the wharf in

1910 and constructed of reinforced concrete, the club was a popular gathering site because of its dance floor, soda fountain, gymnasium, and two-lane bowling alley. In addition to these indoor activities, the guards and their families enjoyed an outdoor baseball diamond, a handball court, a tennis court, and a playground for the children on the southern side of the island. Also popular with the guards and their families was the city of San Francisco. Boats left for the city several times a day, and passage for prison employees was free of charge. In keeping with all of the other activities on the island, security around the wharf was always tight and everyone leaving or arriving on the island was carefully accounted for.

By the beginning of the 1960s, families and prison authorities both could not help noticing the signs of deterioration throughout the island. Repairs to buildings and fences fell behind schedule and two escapes in 1962 prompted another wave of criticism directed against prison officials. With the election of President John F. Kennedy, a more liberal view of prison management began to predominate in the federal prison system. The idea that prisons should be used for punishing inmates came to be seen as outmoded.

In 1961 an engineering survey of the buildings on Alcatraz revealed extensive deterioration and recommended repairs that it was estimated would cost $5,000,000. The survey provided a detailed accounting of all structures, each of which was numbered, described in full, and assessed for action ranging from full restoration to complete demolition. Many recom-

At one time, there were sixty-four children living on the island. Here, children go ashore to spend a few hours in San Francisco.

mendations focused on partial restoration. Much attention focused on structural faults resulting from age, saltwater, and seismic activity. The report also noted recommendations for modernizing all of the electrical, plumbing, and mechanical facilities. This report, along with the changing political landscape of the 1960s, suggested to many living on Alcatraz that the beginning of the end was at hand.

5

FROM PRISON TO NATIONAL PARK

A mere twenty-nine years after the first notorious gangsters arrived in sealed railroad cars in 1934, Alcatraz Island ceased functioning as a federal penitentiary. Soaring costs to house and guard the convict population, relentless structural deterioration caused by saltwater, two escapes in 1962, and the public's growing sense of moral outrage over conditions inside the prison moved Attorney General Robert Kennedy to close Alcatraz on March 21, 1963.

Kennedy did not stand alone in this decision. As early as 1952, the director of the Bureau of Prisons, James Bennett, had recommended the closure of Alcatraz because of its excessive operating costs and difficult location.

According to John Martini, historian for the National Park Service, there were other unofficial reasons for the closure:

> The unspoken truth was the prison had outlived its usefulness. Opened in an era of bootleggers and gun-toting gangsters, Alcatraz had never been the deterrent to crime it had been prophesized to be. Formal orders to shut down the Rock came from Attorney General Robert Kennedy, despite howls of protest from FBI Director J. Edgar Hoover.[16]

Contrary to the myth of Alcatraz, of the 1,545 men the federal government selected for incarceration there, few could boast of having their pictures on a Ten Most Wanted poster and most had not been involved in the sorts of gangland crime that Hoover was trying to deter with the threat of incarceration on Alcatraz. Still, Bureau of Prisons officials believed that Alcatraz had served an important purpose:

The institution [Alcatraz] served an important purpose in taking the strain off our older and greatly overcrowded institutions at Atlanta, Leavenworth, and McNeil Island since it enabled us to move to this smaller, closely guarded institution the escape artists, the big-time racketeers, the inveterate connivers, and those who need protection from other groups.[17]

EXCESSIVE MAINTENANCE COSTS

The saltwater of San Francisco Bay had taken its toll on prison buildings since the inception of the early construction. The cellhouse concrete in particular was rapidly disintegrating, as were all exposed steel supports and the wire fences. Following the escapes in 1962, attention again turned to the condition of the security systems of the island.

A prison inspector finds crumbling pipes in the ventilation shafts. Physical deterioration plus high operating costs eventually led to the abandonment of Alcatraz.

Costs to ferry all of the supplies needed to support the entire prison operation continued to escalate. The costs of feeding and providing for the needs of all of the prisoners and families of the guards could not be justified. Generators for electricity needed thousands of gallons of diesel fuel, as did the fleet of trucks and boats needed for the routine maintenance of the facility. Supplies to repair plumbing, wiring, leaking roofs, warped floors, and flaking paint cost significantly more when loaded aboard boats and then off-loaded at the wharf of Alcatraz.

Alcatraz had always been relatively expensive to operate. One survey comparing the operating costs of Alcatraz with those of other federal prisons during the 1940s showed that the daily cost to house and secure an inmate on Alcatraz was $23.50 a day, two and a half times the $9.27 average for other federal prisons. These costs continued to rise. By the 1960s, the daily cost per prisoner was approaching $100.

THE ESCAPE OF 1946: "THE BLAST-OUT"

On May 2, 1946, six prisoners overpowered cell-block guards, gained access to the gun gallery, and made off with cellhouse keys giving them access to most of the cell block. Labeled the blast-out by the press, these six men succeeded in keeping guards at bay for two days during the most violent escape attempt in the history of the Rock.

All six convicts taking part in the escape faced long sentences and all had criminal histories involving guns and murder. The men chose the time after lunch when prisoners would be returning to their work and the number of guards would be minimal. One of the prisoners, who had dieted for several weeks so as to make himself slender, forced himself through the bars at one end of the gun gallery. He had observed that the vertical bars, although tool-proof, were only six inches apart and could be pried farther. Constructing a simple bar spreader, he separated two of the bars, squeezed through, and overpowered a guard. Taking his keys and guns, the six escapees captured more guards, locking them in cells and killing two of them.

Once they gained control of the entire cell block, they shot their way toward the exercise yard. Their plan was to get to the exercise yard where they could kill the guard in the guard tower, make their way down the cliffs to the bay, and swim to San Francisco. By this time however, sirens were blasting throughout the

PUBLIC CONDEMNATION

Rising costs were only part of the problem. Historian Erwin Thompson recounts in *The Rock: A History of Alcatraz Island, 1847–1972*, the deaths of forty-one prisoners during its twenty-nine years as a federal penitentiary. Seven were shot and killed by guards while trying to escape, two were stabbed by other prisoners, six escaped to the water and were presumed drowned, one committed suicide, and twenty-five died of disease or natural causes. If deaths and escape attempts were not enough to turn people against the Rock, alleged inhumane conditions within the prison's walls were. Moreover, the prison continued to be unpopular among San Francisco's residents.

The citizens of San Francisco had never seen the wisdom of placing a maximum-security prison in the midst of a major met-

prison and off-duty guards came running to prevent the six escapees from gaining access to the exercise yard and the bay.

Trapped in the main cell block, the escapees threatened to kill more guards. To restore order, U.S. Marines arrived on the island to assist in an assault of the cellhouse. Tear gas bombs crashed through the windows sending smoke billowing across the bay. Radio stations interrupted their usual broadcasting to cover the story as reporters chartered boats in hopes of snapping close-up photographs. Crowds of San Franciscans, hearing of the shootout over their radios, flocked to the Golden Gate Bridge to watch and listen for gunfire.

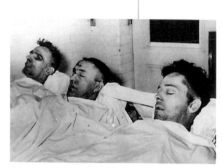

Three of the six "blast-out" escapees, pictured here lying in the morgue, were killed in the disturbance.

With tear gas filling the cell block, most prisoners hid in their cells as guards entered through the roof and other entrances to retake the cell block. In the end, two days after it began, guards shot dead three of the six escapees. Of the three who survived, two were executed in the electric chair in San Quentin for the murder of guards, and the third received a life sentence. Two guards died preventing the escape and fourteen sustained gunshot wounds.

ropolitan area. Citizen groups that had opposed the opening of the federal prison back in 1934 continued to press their opposition. Every time a released prisoner complained to the newspapers about his treatment while on Alcatraz, letters from citizens demanding congressional investigations of prison cruelty flowed into the offices of Cummings and Hoover. Stories of torture and disease brought additional demands that the San Francisco Department of Public Health be allowed to investigate prison conditions. Doctors and psychiatrists demanded visits to Alcatraz to inspect the facilities and to interview inmates. Every attempted escape that was reported to the press reminded the public of the possibility that escapees might run loose in San Francisco.

As time went by, more and more citizen groups lobbied the federal government to close Alcatraz. Stories about the horrors of

THE LAST GREAT ESCAPE

During the federal prison era, thirty-six men tried to escape from Alcatraz in fourteen separate attempts. The best-engineered and most ingenious attempt occurred on June 11, 1962. This escape continues to fascinate people because of the inmates' determination despite astronomical odds against its success.

Working at night, the four convicts involved in the attempt figured that they could remove the six-by-ten-inch vent cover embedded in the rear wall of each cell and thereby gain access to a utility corridor behind their cells. The vent covers were welded to steel reinforcement rods set in the concrete walls and drilling through them would require considerable work. After enlarging the opening to allow a man to crawl through to the utility corridor, the inmate would climb the water pipes to the roof.

The tools at their disposal to penetrate the eight-inch-thick concrete walls were both primitive and ingenious, having been fashioned from spoons taken from the cafeteria and small pieces of metal, including hacksaw blades, stolen from the workshops. Without a doubt, the most ingenious and most effective tool was the drill they fashioned from a stolen fan motor, equipped with drill bits stolen from the workshops. The men first drilled holes through the concrete and then gradually broke off chunks until they had enlarged the openings from six by ten inches to ten by fourteen inches.

The four escapees could not have carried out their plan without the assistance of several other prisoners. Several inmates helped steal drill bits, placing them in hollowed-out pages of library books that were later delivered to the escapees. Others assisted in the assembly of the rubber raft the inmates planned to use to paddle ashore once they got to the water. They also made papier-mâché models of their heads from wire, human hair from the barbershop, newspaper, and paint.

During the day, the four men carefully concealed their work with false cardboard grates painted to match the walls.

solitary confinement, abusive guards, and enforced rules of silence began to raise questions about whether justice was truly being served by keeping the prison open. Although many of these stories were exaggerations, nevertheless the citizens of San Francisco gradually adopted a different attitude toward how a

The concrete that they removed as they enlarged the air vents was crushed and carried outside each morning in their pockets. Finally, they were ready to make their move.

After lights out on June 11, 1962, the four inmates arranged their papier-mâché heads on their pillows and stuffed clothes under their blankets to fool the night guards into believing they were asleep in their bunks. The men then quietly wriggled through the holes they had carved and gathered in the utility corridor behind their cells. One man, underestimating his girth, could not fit through his hole and was forced to stay behind. Once in the utility corridor, the three escapees climbed the water pipes to a ventilator shaft that gave them access to the roof.

On the roof, the three headed to the north end of the cell block, where they shinnied down a drainpipe. Under cover of darkness they slipped past the guard tower and entered the chilly water. Buoyed by homemade flotation devices made from inflated rubber raincoats, they headed north toward Angel Island rather than toward San Francisco.

The papier-mâché ruse gave the men a head start of several hours. Guards did not discover their escape until the next morning when all inmates were required to stand for the head count. The guards on duty recalled banging their wooden clubs on the bars to rouse the men, only to find them in a deep sleep. Finally, one of the guards reached through the bars to shake one of the heads, only to see it fall on the floor. Too late, the sirens sounded.

No one saw the three men again. Most people, including other convicts, presumed that they drowned in the cold, swift waters of San Francisco Bay, although a few cling to the possibility that one or more made it to freedom. A body wearing a blue shirt like those worn by inmates was later recovered along the Pacific coast beyond the bay but it was so badly decomposed that no one could identify it.

prison should function. After a series of confrontations between Alcatraz authorities and medical practitioners, some reforms took place to ease some of the conditions. The hated rule of silence was rescinded and inmates were given greater latitude to listen to more radio stations, play musical instruments, paint or sketch in their cells, and watch movies. Nonetheless, over the years more and more residents of the San Francisco Bay area applied pressure on the federal government to discontinue the use of Alcatraz as a maximum-security prison.

When public condemnation and crippling costs finally closed the maximum-security prison on Alcatraz, no one within the federal government had given much thought to the question of what to do with the twenty-two acre island it owned.

AMERICAN INDIAN OCCUPATION

In April 1963 the federal government officially listed Alcatraz Island as excess government property and in March 1964 held meetings on the island to determine its future. With the closing of the federal penitentiary, questions regarding the future use of the island were posed by residents of San Francisco as well as by politicians in Washington, D.C. One group suggested a statue for the island that would be a West Coast equivalent to the Statue of Liberty. Congress considered this plan but rejected it because of the negative reputation the island had earned as a prison.

Following the meetings in March, a group of Sioux Indians led by Richard McKenzie expressed interest in establishing an American Indian university on the island. John Mitchell, the attorney general of the United States, heard the request but noted that the Sioux did not have a legal claim to the island and rejected their request. Although the Indians filed suit in federal court claiming their right to determine the future of Alcatraz, the court dismissed their suit.

In 1968 the city of San Francisco expressed interest in the island as a park. Soon many citizen groups sprang up suggesting many other uses of Alcatraz that ranged from a casino or a full-fledged resort including hotels and restaurants, to a park or center for the study of the humanities. In July 1969, the government directed the Department of the Interior to research the use of Alcatraz as a recreational area.

Four days after the Department of the Interior took charge of determining the future of the island, a group of fourteen Native Americans landed on the island and claimed it as their territory. Representatives of the government rejected their claim and asked them to leave, which they did, in exchange for a meeting with the government to discuss their claim to the island.

Alcatraz inmates are escorted onto a boat to be transferred to another prison after the closure of Alcatraz in 1963.

No progress was made at this meeting, although the confrontation seemed to have been defused.

On November 9, 1969, a small group of American Indians led by Richard Oakes, a Mohawk Indian, landed on Alcatraz to claim the island for the Indian people. Eleven days following this landing, early in the morning of November 20, a group of approximately ninety Indians representing many Native American tribes occupied Alcatraz and refused to leave when confronted by government officers. They announced their intent to remain until they were allowed to establish a cultural center for Native Americans.

As news of the occupation of Alcatraz spread across the nation and around the world, more Indians joined those already on the island. Activist supporters calling themselves Radio Free Alcatraz broadcasted a fifteen-minute program daily over radio station KPFA in nearby Berkeley to present their point of view to the public. The Indians appointed guards to keep police at a distance, slept in the dormitories previously used by the guards, and cooked their food over open fires within the buildings.

As the occupation stretched into 1970, Indians discussed among themselves a major renovation on the island to accommodate their cultural center. Many buildings would be torn down to make way for new ones and others would be renamed and painted to reflect Native American history and culture.

More Indians had arrived on the island. By now, the number of Indians on Alcatraz had more than doubled. While the Indian activists settled in for a protracted occupation, the Department of the Interior attempted, without success, to negotiate a joint committee of government and Indian representatives to plan for a cultural and educational center on the island. Fearing a trick, the Indians refused the offer. Following other unsuccessful attempts at mediating this difficult situation, the Department of the Interior declared its intention to make Alcatraz into a national park.

FIRE AND DISILLUSIONMENT

Personal tragedy intervened on January 5, 1970, when Oakes's thirteen-year-old stepdaughter fell three floors down a stairwell to

At a meeting for proposed new uses of Alcatraz island, a Sioux Indian representative proposes giving Alcatraz back to the Native Americans for use as a university site.

A Sioux in full regalia (right) leads Indians in a dance to honor "Liberation Day," when a small group of Native Americans took control of the island on November 9, 1969.

her death. Grief-stricken by the young girl's death, Oakes departed from Alcatraz, leaving the Department of Justice and the remaining Indians locked in a stalemate. Meanwhile, the Department of the Interior continued its plans to develop Alcatraz as a national park. In January 1971, congressional leaders introduced a bill that would formally establish Alcatraz as a national park.

Four days following this announcement, fire raged through many significant buildings on the island. Destroyed beyond repair were the warden's quarters, the lighthouse residence, and the post exchange. Attorney General Mitchell blamed the Indians for setting the fires intentionally, although they denied having set them. As the summer of 1970 arrived, living conditions on the island grew more difficult.

All food, water, and other necessities had to be brought to the island by boat at considerable expense to the Indians, and their ability to raise money from a sympathetic public was waning. To raise money, the Indians attempted to lead tours for visitors, but federal government boats blocked the visitors from landing on the island. As the summer wore on, dissension broke out among the Indian leadership, and many left. Different and conflicting points of view were expressed regarding the course that would be most beneficial for the Native Americans. In the midst of their difficulties, many wanted to give up and go home while others believed that they had a moral obligation to continue the struggle on behalf of all Native Americans regardless of the hardships.

As the federal government gradually tightened its grip on Alcatraz, the Native American occupiers turned to a few well-known personalities, hoping that their support for the occupation would generate publicity for their cause. Jane Fonda came to their aid by visiting the island and making speeches in support of the Indians' claim to determine the future of Alcatraz. Folk singer Joan Baez gave a concert supporting the claims of the Native Americans. In spite of this support from a few well-

The old post exchange building was gutted by fire during the occupation of Alcatraz by Native Americans.

known people, financial support for the Indians slowed to a trickle and the federal government showed no signs of relinquishing its ownership of the island.

Finally, on June 11, 1971, the occupation of Alcatraz ended when federal marshals, on orders from President Richard Nixon, landed on the island and removed the last remaining Indians, ten adults and five children. By this time, all other activists had departed. Historian Erwin Thompson quotes the following epilogue from the *San Francisco Chronicle:*

> An aura of sadness hangs over the entire episode for the bravado of its beginnings and its hollow end. It did, however, evoke a sharper understanding of the plight of those American Indians who have been unable to meet the challenges of modern society with the same success enjoyed by many of their fellow Indians. That much can be said for the plus side.[18]

ALCATRAZ'S MOST SIGNIFICANT EVENT

Park ranger Craig Glassner, in an interview on February 27, 1999, expressed the view that the Indian occupation of Alcatraz may have been the most significant historical event in the long history of the island. More significant than the early military fortifications and more important than the era of the federal penitentiary, the brief nineteen-month occupation proved to be the first publicized action taken by American Indians to draw attention to their general economic and social plight. This occupation was the first manifestation of the contemporary Indian civil rights movement.

Dr. Troy Johnson, writing for the Alcatraz Island website sponsored by the National Park Service, had this to say about the value of the Indian occupation of Alcatraz Island:

> The success or failure of the occupation should not be judged by whether the demands of the occupiers were realized. The underlying goals of the Indians on Alcatraz were to awaken the American public to the reality of the plight of the first Americans and to assert the need for Indian self-determination. As a result of the occupation, either directly or indirectly, the official government policy of termination of Indian tribes was ended and a policy

of Indian self-determination became the official U.S. government policy.

During the period the occupiers were on Alcatraz Island, President Nixon returned Blue Lake and 48,000 acres of land to the Taos Indians. Occupied lands near Davis, California, would become home to a Native American university. The occupation of Bureau of Indian Affairs offices in Washington, D.C., would lead to the hiring of Native Americans to work in the federal agency that had such a great effect on their lives.

Alcatraz may have been lost, but the occupation gave birth to a political movement which continues to today.[19]

Although the final decision by the Department of the Interior on the future of Alcatraz was to create a national park, officials have preserved the history of the Indian occupation along with the history of the penitentiary. Visitors to Alcatraz today can learn about the Indian occupation and the history of the Indian struggle there.

ALCATRAZ NATIONAL PARK

On October 12, 1972, two hundred and three years after the first sighting of San Francisco Bay by Gaspar de Portolá, an act of Congress established the Golden Gate National Recreation Area. Fifteen days later President Nixon signed it. Exactly a year later, Alcatraz Island officially opened to the public. Once Alcatraz was placed on the National Register of Historic Places in June 1976, an evaluation of every structure on the island was undertaken to determine what to renovate, what to leave alone, and what to remove.

Categorization was largely based on the historical significance of each structure and its condition. The cellhouse, the dominant structure on the island, has been renovated for public tours. All buildings destroyed by fire during the period of the Indian occupation were bulldozed except for the warden's quarters, the walls of which still stand. All guard towers except one greeting visitors at the dock have been torn down because of excessive rust. Most of the original buildings from the 1800s have been restored and the remainder will be restored as funds become available.

Today, Alcatraz hosts over 1.3 million visitors a year. Some are attracted by its reputation as the prison that once caged notorious cons like Capone, the Birdman, and Machine Gun Kelly. Others want to see where the infamous shootout occurred in 1946 that took the lives of three convicts and two guards. All visitors see the evidence of the American Indian occupation after the prison closed. Although the reasons for visiting are many, few are prepared for the grim reality of the cell blocks as they stare down the drab three-tiered blocks of cells on "Broadway."

The natural beauty of the island and the majestic views it offers of the Golden Gate Bridge, Angel Island, the Bay Bridge, and the San Francisco skyline mesmerize visitors. National Park Service rangers offer guided tours of the massive cellhouse and

The Golden Gate National Recreation Area was established on October 12, 1972. Here, a ferry full of tourists heads toward the island for a visit to the prison.

THE NATIONAL PARK TOUR

For more than twenty-five years, the Alcatraz tour has been a major point of interest for visitors to San Francisco. At one time an island known only to inmates and their guards, today over one million people annually enjoy the short boat ride to the island that offers a very different educational and enjoyable historical experience.

The tour begins with a boat ride from Fisherman's Wharf that provides the same first view of the island that nearly all prisoners saw as they made the 1.5-mile crossing. Docking at the same wharf used when Alcatraz was a penitentiary, visitors disembark to climb the twisting road up to the parade grounds, the lighthouse, and the cellhouse. From this vantage point visitors gain sparkling views of the San Francisco wharf and skyline. New prisoners never saw this panorama, however, because they were led into the cellhouse by a back entry.

As visitors look about before entering the cellhouse, they see the remains of several burned-out buildings damaged in the early 1970s during the Indian occupation. They also see the parade ground first used when the U.S. Army controlled the prison and which later became a baseball field for the children of guards when the federal government controlled the prison.

Visitors may choose, as one option, outdoor interpretive walks offered throughout the day by National Park Service rangers that cover a variety of topics including military history, famous inmates, escapes, natural history, and the Indian occupation. The other option is the self-guided tour through the cellhouse and other points of historical interest. There is also a thirty-five minute recorded tour that corresponds to a walk through the cellhouse.

Several exhibits are located behind the theater that present the various periods of Alcatraz's history, including the U.S. penitentiary (1934–1963) and the military history (1850–1933). A new video, "We Hold the Rock," presents the story of the occupation by Indians of All Tribes (1969–1971). There is also an excellent bookstore near the dock that is filled with memorabilia, films, videos, and books about the island's rich history.

scenic grounds of the island seven days a week. Alcatraz has also become a protected habitat for several endangered birds that have been found nesting on the island. For that reason, a good portion of the nature trails of the island are now off-limits to visitors.

The perception of Alcatraz as a maximum-security prison is slowly yielding to one of Alcatraz as a beautiful national park where breaking waves, dazzling vistas, and resurgent flora dominate visitors' memories of their visit. Vines of many types

Every year, roughly a million tourists flock to the now-empty federal penitentiary on Alcatraz. Many of the visitors who wander the abandoned halls that once housed some of America's most dangerous men get at least some sense of what life was like there.

have wrapped themselves around the disintegrating concrete walks and handrails, while trees planted during the beginning of the federal prison era have reached maturity, providing a verdant canopy for local sea birds.

The Alcatraz that Gaspar de Portolá discovered by land and that Juan Manuel de Ayala discovered by sea is forever lost but, with time and proper conservancy by the National Park Service, Alcatraz may well again become Isla de los Alcatraces.

Notes

Chapter 1: Early History

1. Miguel Costansó, *The Discovery of San Francisco Bay: The Portolá Expedition: The Diary of Miguel Costansó*, ed. Peter Browning. Lafayette, CA: Great West Books, 1992, p. xvii.

2. Costansó, *The Discovery of San Francisco Bay*, p. 119.

3. John A. Martini, *Fortress Alcatraz*. Kailua, HI: Pacific Monograph, 1990, p. 15.

4. Martini, *Fortress Alcatraz*, p. 22.

Chapter 2: Military Prison

5. Quoted in Martini, *Fortress Alcatraz*, p. 66.

6. Erwin N. Thompson, *The Rock: A History of Alcatraz Island, 1847–1972*. Denver: U.S. Department of the Interior, 1979, p. 264.

7. Quoted in Thompson, *The Rock*, p. 305.

Chapter 3: Federal Maximum-Security Prison

8. Quoted in Joel Gazis-Sax, "Alcatraz—The Warden Johnston Years" website. www.notfrisco.com/alcatraz/index.html.

9. Quoted in *San Francisco Chronicle*, December 13, 1934.

10. Paul J. Madigan, *Institution Rules & Regulations: United States Penitentiary Alcatraz, California*. San Francisco: Golden Gate National Parks Association, 1983, p.1.

Chapter 4: Keeping Inmates and Their Guards Secure

11. Thompson, *The Rock*, p. 382.

12. Frank Heaney and Gay Machado, *Inside the Walls of Alcatraz*. Palo Alto, CA: Bull, 1997, p. 42.

13. Quoted in Thompson, *The Rock*, p. 367.

14. Quoted in Jolene Babyak, *Eyewitness on Alcatraz: Life on the Rock as Told by the Guards, Families, and Prisoners*. Berkeley, CA: Ariel Vamp Press, 1988, p. 1.

15. Quoted in Babyak, *Eyewitness on Alcatraz*, p. 62.

Chapter 5: From Prison to National Park

16. Martini, *Fortress Alcatraz*, p. 139.

17. Thompson, *The Rock*, p. 414.

18. Thompson, *The Rock*, p. 473.

19. National Park Service website. www.nps.gov/alcatraz/indian.4html.

FOR FURTHER READING

Jolene Babyak, *Eyewitness on Alcatraz: Life on the Rock as Told by the Guards, Families, and Prisoners.* Berkeley, CA: Ariel Vamp Press, 1988. Babyak's remembrances as the daughter of an associate warden growing up on Alcatraz.

Eugene R. Hart, *A Guide to the California Gold Rush.* San Francisco: Freewheel, 1993. This book puts the reader in the shoes of those who participated in the great rush to California. Of special interest is the never before published diary of Charles Brown, how miners extracted the gold from the ground, and a nice sampling of the gold rush towns that one can still visit today.

Frank Heaney and Gay Machado, *Inside the Walls of Alcatraz.* Palo Alto, CA: Bull, 1997. Heaney provides some interesting insights into the life of the guards on Alcatraz. The reading is light and provides glimpses of the everyday relationships between guards and inmates.

Jim Quillen, *Alcatraz from Inside.* San Francisco: Golden Gate National Park Association, 1991. Quillen's book, from the point of view of a prisoner, covers the period from 1942 to 1952. He details the 1946 blast-out and describes the personalities of many guards as well as inmates.

WORKS CONSULTED

BOOKS

James V. Bennett, *I Chose Prison*. New York: Knopf, 1970. A revealing insight into Bennett's views on how prisons operate and their function. Bennett expresses many interesting and unexpected views on how best to run prisons and on humane treatment of convicts.

Miguel Costansó, *The Discovery of San Francisco Bay: The Portolá Expedition: The Diary of Miguel Costansó*. Ed. Peter Browning. Lafayette, CA: Great West Books, 1992. Fascinating reading for the early history of California. Browning provides the diary in both English and Spanish.

Paul J. Madigan, *Institution Rules & Regulations: United States Penitentiary Alcatraz, California*. San Francisco: Golden Gate National Parks Association, 1983. The actual set of rules and regulations handed to each new Alcatraz inmate. Stark and crude, it sets forth what was expected of each new arrival in 1956.

John A. Martini, *Fortress Alcatraz*. Kailua, HI: Pacific Monograph, 1990. Martini's work spans the entire history of Alcatraz but focuses on the period when it functioned as a military prison between 1848 and 1934. He provides a masterful profile of early fortifications and armament, complete with photographs and maps. This is the most thorough discussion available of Alcatraz as a military fort and prison.

Erwin N. Thompson, *The Rock: A History of Alcatraz Island, 1847–1972*. Denver: U.S. Department of the Interior, 1979. The definitive history of Alcatraz. Written for the historian and the scholar, it remains the basis for all following studies. Unfortunately out of print, it also contains an extraordinary bibliography.

INTERNET SOURCES

Joel Gazis-Sax, "Alcatraz—The Warden Johnston Years," 1998. www.notfrisco.com/alcatraz/index.html. This website provides an extraordinary wealth of information on the history of Alcatraz as a prison. It focuses on the federal prison period between 1934 and 1963. The website's message is that the treatment of prisoners was inhumane and unjustified, a view only partially supported by fact. An excellent accumulation of diverse information.

The National Park Service, Golden Gate National Recreation Area, "Alcatraz Island," 1998. www.nps.gov/alcatraz. This website is maintained by the National Park Service to provide visitors with a history of the island and visitor information.

Index

Picture Credits

About the Author

James Barter received his undergraduate degree in history and classics at the University of California (Berkeley), followed by graduate studies in ancient history and archaeology at the University of Pennsylvania. Mr. Barter has taught European history as well as the Latin and Greek languages.

Mr. Barter currently lives in Rancho Santa Fe, California, with his daughter Kalista who, at fourteen, has a promising acting career. His older daughter, Tiffany, is a classic violinist with the Kansas City Symphony.

Mr. Barter is well known for his slide presentations at local universities, bookstores, and museums throughout San Diego County.